Garden Terms Simplified

Garden Terms Simplified

by
A. J. HUXLEY, M.A.

DAVID & CHARLES: NEWTON ABBOT

ISBN 0 7153 5366 7

First published in 1962
by W. H. Collingridge Limited
Second edition published in 1971
by David & Charles (Publishers) Limited

© A. J. Huxley 1971

Reproduced and Printed in Great Britain by
Redwood Press Limited Trowbridge & London
for David & Charles (Publishers) Limited
South Devon House Newton Abbot Devon

INTRODUCTION

Most of the entries in this book appeared week by week as a series in *Amateur Gardening*, between 1957 and 1961, under the heading 'Garden Terms'. It was a natural follow-up to publish the series in book form. By the addition of cross-references and a number of new entries, a veritable pocket dictionary has been created, which includes not only most of the technical words and jargon likely to be met in gardening literature, but many of the more commonly used botanical terms. The text has been kept as simple as possible and almost every item is accompanied by a drawing, on the principle that a picture is usually worth several dozen words.

These drawings are almost entirely the work of Miss Dora Ratman, who prepared them week by week according to my requirements; a few were obtained from other sources.

London, 1971   A. J. HUXLEY

ACID. *See* Calcicole.

ACUMINATE. Tapering to a long narrow point with its sides curved inwards; usually applied to leaves.

ACUTE. Ending in a sharp point, with straight or outward-curving sides; usually applied to leaves.

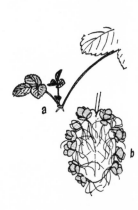

ADVENTITIOUS. A growth or organ produced by a plant at a point where such growths do not normally occur is termed adventitious. The examples illustrated are the roots on a strawberry runner (a), and the plantlets on the leaves of many species of bryophyllum and kalanchoe (b). Other examples are roots produced by cuttings, which would not occur if the shoot was left on the parent; roots at the tips of blackberry canes; and the shoots that appear on pollarded or cut trees, despite the absence of buds there previously. *See also* Joint; Pollard; Runner; Stolon; Sucker; Viviparous; Water Shoot.

AERIAL ROOT. Any root produced above ground level is known as aerial. Such roots are of two main kinds. Many climbing plants, such as philodendron, *Ficus pumila*, and the ivy illustrated, cling to trees, walls, etc., with them. Plants which naturally live on trees (epiphytes), without contact with the ground, also cling with aerial roots, but in these cases the roots are specially adapted to absorb atmospheric moisture as well. *See also* Epiphyte.

AIR LAYERING. Also known as Chinese layering after its inventors, this is the ideal way of rooting woody plants, either when they have become too tall and leggy, as often happens with room plants, or when they are difficult to strike from cuttings. To make an air layer either make a slit about 1 in. long into the stem, from below upwards (a), and push a sliver of wood into it to keep it open (b), or cut and remove a ring of bark about ½ in. wide (c), in each case at the point where roots are wanted. Dust the cut with a hormone root-forming powder if available. Next, bind a handful of moist sphagnum moss or peat around the cut with a few turns of thread (d); then surround this with a piece of polythene sheet (or a polythene bag cut open), overlapping it well and tying firmly top and bottom (e, f). A few weeks after roots show through the moss, cut the stem below the moss ball (g) and carefully pot up the new plant. The old stem can be cut back nearly to soil level to encourage new growth from the base.

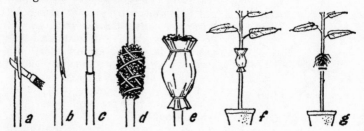

ALATE. *See* Wing.

ALKALINE. *See* Calcicole.

ALPINE. Strictly, a plant native to mountains; in practice, any plant suitable for the rock garden.

ALTERNATE. Applied to leaves occurring singly on a. stem at different heights, alternating, at least more or less, from one side to the other; a term that is often used in keys to aid identification in contrast to leaves in pairs opposite each other, or in whorls. *See also* Opposite; Whorl.

AMPLEXICAUL. *See* Clasping.

ANEMONE-CENTRED. A term applied to composite flowers, especially chrysanthemums (illustrated) and dahlias, in which the tubular florets of the central disk are enlarged so that they form a kind of cushion, often of a contrasting colour among the flat ray florets. Certain peonies and camellias are sometimes called anemone-flowered, but these are cases of petalody. *See also* Composite, Petal.

ANNUAL. A plant which grows from seed to maturity in one year (not necessarily a calendar year) and then dies.

ANTHER. The anther is the part of the flower which produces pollen, the male sex cells of the plant. The anther, which is often large and decorative as in the lily (a), is usually carried on a slender stem called the filament, the whole being known as a stamen; but in some cases the anthers are small and may even adhere directly to the petals, as in anchusa (b). (The flower is shown cut open.) In a few special cases, including the orchids, the pollen is carried in different ways. *See also* Column; Stamen.

ARCURE. A system of training fruit trees in the vertical plane, popular in France, and with ornamental possibilities. The sketch shows the system clearly; the topmost bud of each arch is allowed to develop, while the arching checks the upward flow of sap and so increases fruitfulness.

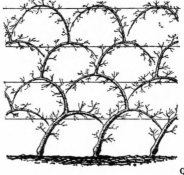

ARISTATE. *See* Awn.

AROID. Any plant belonging to the family Araceae, which includes our wild lords-and-ladies, the arum or calla lily (zantedeschia) (*top*), anthurium (*below*), philodendron and monstera. These are characterised by an inflorescence consisting of a cylindrical spadix, densely packed with tiny flowers, the male towards the top and the female below, and having a single bract known as a spathe at the base. This is almost

always the showy part of the plant, and may be flattish, as in the anthurium, or more or less rolled around the spadix, as in the arum lily and lords-and-ladies. *See also* Bract; Spathe.

ARTICULATE. Jointed; *see* Joint.

AWL-SHAPED. A term usually applied to leaves, indicating resemblance to a cobbler's awl with its sharp, up-turned point. The leaves illustrated are the juvenile ones of the Norfolk Island pine, *Araucaria excelsa*.

AWN. A thread-like termination to a fruit, seed or leaf; the word is most commonly applied to the 'beard' on the seeds of many grasses and cereals, as in the barley illustrated. The 'beak' on cranesbill fruits is another type of awn. The awn is, probably, basically a dispersal mechanism, attaching itself to the coats of animals or in some cases light enough to enable the seed to be carried in the wind. A plant with awns may be described as awned or aristate, which is synonymous and is sometimes Latinised as a specific name, as in *Aloe aristata*. *See also* Beard.

AXIL. The angle between a leaf or leaf-stalk and the stem from which it is growing. Any bud in this position, as shown in the camellia illustrated, is known as an axillary bud. Buds of this type are used in the grafting operation known as budding. *See also* Budding.

BASAL. A word often used, especially in botanical works, to differentiate the lower leaves of a plant, which may differ considerably from those on the stem. In the example illustrated, *Erigeron alpinus*, the basal leaves are arranged in a loose rosette. Basal is, in the botanical sense, more or less synonymous with radical.

BEARD. A growth of hairs, in particular that which occurs on the lower petals or falls of some irises. The long awns on some cereals and ornamental grasses are also known as beards.

This drawing also shows the up-standing petals or standards of the bearded iris. *See also* Awn.

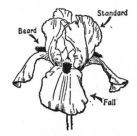

BEDDING PLANT. A plant used for temporary display which is planted or 'bedded out' in quantities, often after being grown almost to flowering stage elsewhere. Examples are salvias, pelargoniums, cherry pie.

BELL GLASS. A large glass jar shaped like a bell which was developed in France by market gardeners who used it for intensive cultivation of early crops, placing it over individual plants or groups of small plants. The French word for bell glass is cloche, a word which has in Britain come to be applied to the continuous structures constructed of glass panes and wire. Bell glasses are now practically unobtainable in this country, the lantern cloche being the nearest approach where it is wanted to maintain a very close, humid atmosphere over cuttings. A large jam jar makes a good substitute. *See also* Cloche.

BERRY. Botanically, a berry is a succulent fruit in which the usually hard seeds are embedded in pulp and protected only by an outer fleshy wall formed from the ovary, as opposed to the drupe or stone fruit in which the seed is enclosed in a hard coat as well as outer pulp. In common parlance the term is very loosely applied; thus, raspberries and blackberries are botanically compound drupes, though gooseberries (illustrated) and currants are true berries. Other true berries include pomegranate, melon, cucumber,

tomato, orange, grape and date (illustrated)—in the latter the hard 'stone' is all seed, not a hard coat around a seed. The banana is is another berry, though the edible kinds seldom produce seed. *See also* Drupe.

BIENNIAL. A plant which takes two seasons to grow from seed to maturity and then dies.

BLIND. A term applied to plants when loss of the growing point has stopped growth, as often occurs in seedlings of cabbages and other brassicas, especially after attack by the cabbage root fly maggot. Plants thus damaged will not make a new growing point nor further growth, and should be discarded.

BOLTING. The premature production of flowers in a vegetable. All vegetables eventually flower if left in the ground, but are normally used before that. Particularly in hot, dry weather or after a severe check, vegetables such as lettuces (illustrated) may form no hearts at all or run to flower shortly after hearting.

BONSAI. A method of dwarfing plants, usually trees, by special root and shoot pruning and often complex training, invented by the Chinese and Japanese.

BOTTLE GARDEN. *See* Wardian Case.

BOTTLE GRAFT. *See* Inarching.

BOTTOM HEAT. Heat applied from below, especially in a frame, sometimes for growing plants such as melons or cucumbers, or for the propagation of many plants from cuttings or seeds. The oldest method is to rest a frame on a bed of decomposing manure (a)—a hotbed. The most modern systems use electrically warmed cables laid under the soil (b). It is possible to provide bottom heat in a greenhouse by making a bed of soil around a hot water pipe (c). On a small scale self-contained propagators may make use of electric heaters or (d) a small oil heater. *See also* Frame.

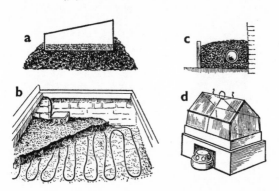

BRACT. A leaf or leaf-like structure at the base of a flower stalk or the stem of a flower cluster, or forming part of the flower head itself (as in the involucre of composite plants). They are often ordinary foliage leaves but may be large and brightly coloured or reduced to small green scales. In the wood spurge illustrated (*right*) there are three kinds of bract (arrowed). Another euphorbia, the poinsettia, is notable for the large scarlet bracts which surround

the insignificant flowers. The dogwoods (cornus) (*top, left*) usually have four petal-like bracts surrounding the small flower-head and in the pocket handkerchief tree (davidia) (*below, left*) there are two large white bracts of different shapes. The showy part of an arum lily is technically a bract. *See also* Aroid; Involucre; Nut.

BREAK. In gardening, a branch or fork. The term is especially used by chrysanthemum and carnation growers, who pinch out the tips of their plants at an early stage in order to induce them to break, that is, to produce lateral side-shoots (as arrowed) which otherwise they would not do. If a rooted chrysanthemum cutting is left to its own devices it will usually, after a time, produce an abortive bud at the top of the stem. This prevents further lengthening of the stem and forces it to produce side-shoots. Hence this abortive bud is often known as the break bud. In another and more general sense 'breaking' is, of course, commonly used to describe opening buds. For 'broken' tulips, *see* Feathered.

    The word break is also sometimes used to denote a mutation, or sport, *which see.*

BREASTWOOD. Shoots which grow forward from vertically trained fruit trees or shrubs, and are thus difficult to train. Breastwood must normally be removed from fruit trees when summer-pruning.

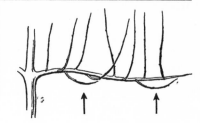

BRISTLY. *See* Hairy.

BROKEN. *See* Feathered; Virus.

BRUTTING. Fracturing one-year fruit tree shoots in summer, so that the ends are left hanging but still attached to the tree. This is sometimes done to prevent late summer growth after summer pruning in a wet summer. Brutted shoots are cut back a few buds below the break in the autumn. Brutting is a typical feature of hazel-nut cultivation.

BUD. A bud is an embryo shoot, flower or flower cluster. A study of buds is often very useful to the gardener, who can often judge from them the progress of growth, whether any pruning is necessary and, if so, how and when to do it. The fruit grower in particular must learn the difference between growth buds (*centre*) and so-called fruit buds (*left*) which are really flower buds. Growth buds can sometimes develop into fruit buds. The peach sometimes has triple buds (*right*), consisting of two fruit and one growth buds. A terminal bud is one at the tip of a shoot, and an axillary bud one found in the axil of a leaf. In the normal course of

events many buds do not develop, but if the upper parts of a trunk or stem are destroyed these latent or dormant buds will become active and produce growth. *See also* Axil; Eye; Nicking; Pruning.

BUDDING. A method of grafting widely used with all kinds of fruit trees and with roses (illustrated). Budding is usually done in summer when the plant is in full growth. Plump buds are cut from the middle portion of firm young shoots (*top, left*); a T-shaped cut is made in the bark of the stock (*top, right*) into which the bud, its 'shield' of bark now cut squarely across as shown, is slipped (*below, left*). The 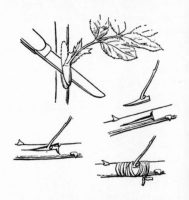 graft is now bound with raffia (*below, right*). *See also* Axil; Grafting; Scion; Sucker.

BULB, BULBIL. A bulb may be regarded as a much modified bud, usually formed underground, with fleshy scales or swollen leaf bases which store food during a resting period. In its centre is an embryo shoot and often, as shown in the sectioned tulip bulb (*left*) a complete embryo flower. This section also shows an axillary bud. Some bulbs are composed of overlapping scales, as in many lilies (*centre*).

A bulbil is a miniature bulb which some plants, such as the tiger lily (*right*), form on their stems. If grown on these become full-size bulbs.

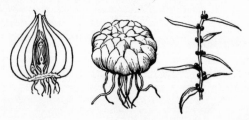

The word bulb and its adjective bulbous are often loosely applied, for convenience, to any kind of plant with a specialised fleshy rootstock, including corms, tubers and rhizomes (*which see*).

CACTUS. Any member of the natural order Cactaceae. A term often misused to mean any fleshy plant. The correct word to use in this general sense is succulent; almost all cacti (plural) are succulents but not all succulents are cacti. Cacti commonly have spines and are very often globular (*above*) or cylindrical, and seldom have leaves, though in various genera such as the epiphyllums and zygocactus (*below*, *left*) the stems may  appear leaf-like. The most primitive cacti, such as pereskia (*below*, *right*) are not succulent and have ordinary leaves. *See also* Spine; Succulent.

CALCICOLE, CALCIFUGE. A calcifuge plant, to start with the more commonly used of these terms, is one which dislikes lime or chalk in any form and, as with the heaths (*Erica cinerea* illustrated, *right*), rhododendrons and other members of the family Ericaceae, may die in limy soil. The camellia (*centre*) is one of the plants most sensitive to lime. Calcicole plants enjoy lime in the soil, though there are very few plants which must have it. Most alpines like lime, and the scabious (*left*) certainly grows much better where lime is present. Limy soils are alkaline, and non-limy ones acid (in general terms); the degree of acidity or alkalinity is measured on what is known as the pH scale, below pH 7 being acid, above, alkaline.

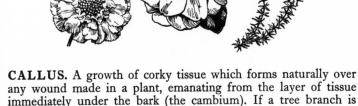

CALLUS. A growth of corky tissue which forms naturally over any wound made in a plant, emanating from the layer of tissue immediately under the bark (the cambium). If a tree branch is cut off the callus will gradually cover the wound (illustrated) and new bark eventually forms over it. In a similar way a callus is formed at the base of cuttings, and it is partly from the callus that new roots are produced. They may also be formed from the cells immediately above the callus. In grafts the cut surfaces of stock and scion both produce callus tissue which eventually join and seal the union. *See also* Grafting; Scion; Sucker.

CALYX. A flower is composed of much modified leaves, and the outer series of these is known as the calyx (plural calyces), each separate lobe or segment being called a sepal. Sometimes the sepals and petals are very similar, as in cacti, water lilies, true lilies and tulips, but usually they are different, the sepals often having a protective function to the inner parts of the flower (rose illustrated, *left*). The sepals may be joined into a tube or cup, or may be

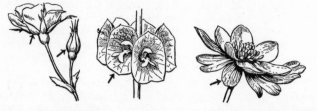

separate. Commonly the calyx is small and green, but in some cases, as in the anemones and clematis, where there are often no petals at all, the calyx may be coloured and decorative. Other examples of decorative calyx include the winter aconite (eranthis) (*right*), and the shell flower (molucella) (*centre*). *See also* Perianth; Sepal.

CAMPANULATE. Literally, bell-shaped; applied to flowers of this form. The harebell family, Campanulaceae, and genus, Campanula, are so called because so many of the species have campanulate flowers.

CANESCENT. *See* Hairy.

CAPITATE. In heads or very compact clusters.

CAPSULE. A capsule is a dry fruit which splits or opens to discharge its seeds, and which consists of several carpels joined together as in the poppy (*left*), iris (*right*) and foxglove. The follicle of peonies and monkshood, and pod of peas, are varieties of capsule.

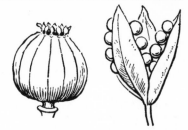

CARPEL. A carpel is one female unit of a flower, consisting of stigma, style and ovary. One or more carpels constitute the pistil,

which is the total female part of the flower, as shown in the heavy portion of the sketch of a sectioned buttercup flower (*left*; one carpel arrowed and magnified *at right*). *See also* Pistil; Stigma.

CATKIN. A particular kind of flower spike, usually pendulous, of stalkless flowers which often have no petals and are surrounded with small scale-like bracts; the flowers are almost always of one sex only, and the male and female catkins may be of quite different shapes, as in the hazel, one of the most familiar catkin-bearing trees. *Garrya elliptica* (illustrated) is an ornamental example; the male form has much longer catkins than the female. The willow is a tree with erect catkins, of which the male is the familiar 'pussy' willow.

CHIMAERA. A plant in which two separate kinds of tissue exist, usually as a result of a sport or mutation. There are several types of chimaera. In one the skin layer is of one character and the inner tissue of another, as in the potato Golden Wonder, which has a russet skin. If propagated from buds induced to form in the flesh, the resulting tubers are of the smooth-skinned variety Langworthy.

19

Some variegated plants are chimaeras with one layer of tissue colourless, which looks white in the absence of the other, green layer. In *Sansevieria trifasciata* the yellow-edged form known as laurentii (*below, left*) is a chimaera, which will not reproduce from cuttings; these revert to the plain form (*below, right*). Sometimes apples (*top*) and chrysanthemums have sectors of a different colour, in which one kind of tissue lies alongside the other and not over or under it.

Some chimaeras are produced by grafting; the most notable example of this is *Laburnocytisus adamii*, created by grafting laburnum on *Cytisus purpureus*. The stock tissue becomes mingled with that of the scion, so that the tree produces, at random, laburnum growth and flowers, broom growth and flowers, and intermediate growth with laburnum-like flowers which are, however, purplish like those of the broom. *See also* Grafting; Sport; Variegated.

CHINESE LAYERING. *See* Air Layering.

CHROMOSOME. The chromosomes are microscopic rod-like bodies found in all living cells. They contain the numerous genes which are the units of inheritance and control the development and appearance of the plant. In ordinary cells the chromosomes divide when the cells do so, so that the number in each cell remains the same. However, the divisions by which male and female sex cells are formed result in each cell having only half the basic chromosome complement. Thus, when two sex cells fuse at fertilisation, each contributes its half share, so that the original chromosome number is restored and each parent contributes half its characteristics to the offspring.

Each species of plant (and animal) has a characteristic basic number of chromosomes, which may, however, be altered both accidentally in nature or by artificial means such as the application

of colchicine or atomic irradiation. Plants with the normal chromosome count are called diploids (abbreviated 2x), whereas abnormal ones are called polyploids. The latter usually look different and may be bigger and more valuable for garden purposes. Those with twice the normal chromosome complement are known as tetraploids (4x). Some fruit trees have one and a half times the normal number; these triploids (3x) produce very little fertile pollen and must have a pollinator. *See also* Hybrid; Sport; Tetraploid; Triploid.

CILIATE. Fringed with hairs; the word is derived from the Latin cilium, an eyelash, and is usually applied to leaves.

CLADODE. A stem which has taken on the function and often the appearance of a leaf. The fact that they are stems is demonstrated by their carrying the flowers, which leaves never do. The most familiar example is the Butcher's Broom, *Ruscus aculeatus* (*left*). In *Colletia cruciata* (*right*) the true leaves are almost microscopic, while

the thorny stem ends carry out the leaf functions. Cladodes, or phylloclades as they are sometimes known, are usually tough and hard, and are usually adaptations to dry conditions. Sometimes, as in some brooms, there are neither leaves nor leaf-like structures, and here the whole stem is green and carries out the leaf functions. These are known as switch plants.

CLASPING. A term applied almost always to stemless leaves which partly or entirely surround the stem from which they grow. The Latin derivation equivalent to this, sometimes used in specific names, is amplexicaul.

CLOCHE. A French word meaning bell, originally applied to the bell glass, and now referring to its development the continuous cloche. This is composed of glass panes held together with clips or wires, which make a rigid structure when fitted together and can be readily dismantled. There are many patterns, shapes and sizes

21

available. Shown below are the tent (*top, left*), tomato cloche (*top, right*), low barn (*centre*), large barn (*below, left*) and small lantern cloche (*below, right*). The word is also applied to any readily movable wire- or metal-framed structure covered with glass or plastic. *See also* Bell Glass.

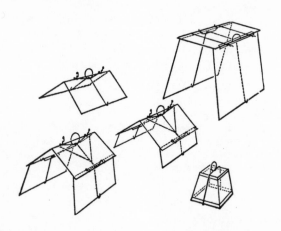

CLONE. A collective term for all the plants vegetatively produced at any time from one original parent or from the vegetative offspring

of that parent. Thus all cuttings, layers or runners from, say, one carnation or one strawberry plant form a clone, but not plants raised from seed from one parent. Plants from one clone are the same in all botanical respects, with certain exceptions where juvenile growth is used for propagation.

CLOVE. A term generally used to describe the young bulbs produced by shallots (*left*) or garlic (*right*); in the latter case they are gathered under the outer skin. The word is also applied to an aromatic spice in the form of the flower buds of a tree, *Eugenia aromatica*; and to kinds of carnation with strong fragrance which are known as clove-scented or sometimes just as cloves.

COLUMN. In orchids, the female pistil and male stamens are united into the column, which is shown speckled in the cymbidium

illustrated. The pollen is not carried in anthers as in most other plants, but in pollinia or pollen-masses.

The term is also occasionally applied to the united tube of stamens that surrounds the pistil in the mallow family. *See also* Anther; Pistil; Stamen.

COMPOSITE. Any member of the daisy family, *Compositae*— the largest family of flowering plants with over 900 genera and 14,000 species—in which many small individual flowers, or florets, are united in one head. The florets are fixed on to the fleshy termination of the flower stem, which is called the receptacle, and this compound flower has a common calyx, called the involucre, surrounding the whole. The calyx of each floret is combined with the ovary, often in the form of a pappus consisting of feathery hairs, as in dandelion seeds, or of chaffy scales.

The florets of composites are of two different kinds. Both may be found together, the tubular ones massed in the centre to form the disk, and the ligulate or strap-shaped ones around these forming the ray, as in the moon daisy, *Chrysanthemum leucanthemum* (1). For this reason the two kinds of floret are often called disk (d) and ray (r) florets respectively. Sometimes the flower is entirely composed of tubular florets, as in the cornflower, *Centaurea cyanus* (2), and sometimes entirely of strap-shaped, as in the hawkweeds, *Hieracium spp.* (3).

One of these florets is shown separately to show the pappus (p) and ovary (o). *See also* Involucre.

COMPOST. *See* Humus.

CONE. The clustered flowers or fruits of some conifers (pines, larches, spruces, etc.). The male and female cones are separate, the females developing into the familiar, usually hard cones, the scales of which usually open to release the seeds. These may have a papery, one-sided wing, and are then dispersed by wind, but others, as in the Stone Pine, resemble a small nut, and can in fact be eaten. In some cases the cones remain closed and only release the seeds through rotting, animals eating them, or even fire. Some cones point downwards when mature, as in *Pinus ayaca-huite* (*right*), and others remain upright, as in the cedar of Lebanon (*left*). The yew, maidenhair tree and some other conifers do not have cones. Other groups of plants which have cone-like structures are the cycads and the horsetails, the latter producing spores, not seeds.

CONIFER. A general term for cone-bearing trees such as pine and spruce, but sometimes used as an equivalent to Coniferae, the original botanical name for a group now considered to consist of eight families, of which a few (e.g. gingko) do not have cones.

CORDATE. Heart-shaped: a term usually applied to leaves with a pair of rounded lobes at the base. When the word is part of a longer description, as cordate-ovate, it is to these lobes only that the term applies.

CORDON. A normally branching plant which is restricted to a single stem, or occasionally two or three stems, by appropriate cultural methods. It is most commonly applied to fruit trees (apple cordons illustrated) and soft fruits (the side-growths of all these restricted to spurs), and to sweet peas. *See also* Spur.

CORM, CORMEL, CORMLET. A storage organ which takes the form of a compact, thickened stem, having no separate layers as in a bulb; there are a few protective papery scales outside. The most familiar corms are those of gladiolus (illustrated) and crocus. The tiny corms that may form round the base of the parent, as shown, are called cormlets or sometimes cormels.

COROLLA. The corolla is a general term applied to the petals of a flower, or at least to the inner whorl of floral leaves, as opposed to the sepals. The corolla is usually, but not always, the the most showy part of the bloom. It may be of many shapes, such as the trumpet of *Gentiana acaulis* (*left*) or the two lips of antirrhinums (*right*). It may be in one piece or of several petals. *See also* Lip; Perianth; Petal.

CORONA. A term applied to any outgrowth developed on the corolla or perianth of a flower, and often called the crown. It separates the corolla from its anthers in the daffodil family, where it forms the cup or trumpet (*left*). In the milkweed family (asclepiads) it is actually an outgrowth from the staminal area, as in

25

Stapelia variegata (right). The radiating filaments of a passion flower are also called the corona or crown. *See also* Cup; Trumpet; Perianth.

CORYMB. A more or less flat-topped flower cluster, in which the usually small flowers or flower-heads are all carried at about the same height, but the flower stalks spring from the main stem at different points, as opposed to an umbel in which they radiate from one point. To the botanist the corymb is a modified raceme. *Achillea ptarmica* is illustrated.

COTYLEDON. A seed leaf. The flowering plants are divided into the two big classes Dicotyledons (seedlings with two seed leaves) and Monocotyledons (with one seed leaf). Cotyledons usually appear above ground, though in the pea and some other plants they remain below. They are usually quite different in appearance to the adult leaves. It is when the cotyledons are fully developed, but before the first adult leaves have appeared, that seedlings are best pricked out. At this stage there is less danger of damaging the root system. The gardener learns to distinguish

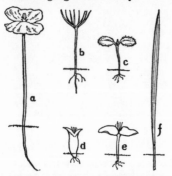

between seedlings of weeds and cultivated plants, so that he can destroy the one kind and preserve or transplant the other. Illustrated are seedlings in the cotyledon stage of (a) beech, (b) oriental spruce, (c) dog rose, (d) cereus cactus, (e) prickly pear, (f) date. The last is a monocotyledon, (b) is a conifer, and the remainder are dicotyledons. *See also* Pricking Out.

CRENATE, CRENULATE. *See* Toothed; Undulate.

CRISTATE. A word meaning, literally, crested, or cockscomb-shaped, which is applied to certain plants showing this type of fasciation, or abnormal growth in one plane. In most plants any kind of fasciation is more curious than beautiful, and rarely possible to propagate, though in the celosias the crested forms of

C. argentea are reproducible from seed and designated by the varietal name cristata (a). In the ferns and the cacti such variations are prized by collectors, and there are many cristate varieties in these two classes of plant, which can be reproduced by division or, with cacti, by cuttings or grafting. The typical crested fern has a spreading tassel-shaped end to the frond (b), while cristate cacti exhibit a vast variety of shapes, basically fan-like (c), often convoluted when growth in one plane at the top of the plant greatly exceeds growth at the base (d), or producing a vast number of tiny heads (e). This latter type of growth is often technically referred to as monstrous. *See also* Fasciation.

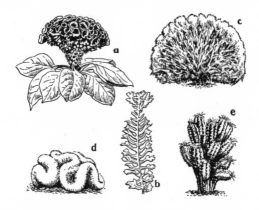

CROSS. *See* Hybrid.

CROWN, CROWN BUD. A word with several horticultural applications. In general, it is used to indicate the upper part of a rootstock from which shoots grow, and to which they die back in autumn, as in plants with a fleshy or woody rootstock like the peony, lupin, delphinium, dahlia (*left, overleaf*), rhubarb and so on. It is sometimes loosely used to mean the whole of a rootstock, especially when this is lifted for forcing, as in rhubarb or seakale.

Secondly, the word is synonymous with corona when referring to flowers in which this tubular or cup-shaped outgrowth from the petals occurs, notably daffodils.

Thirdly, the term is used by chrysanthemum growers to denote a particular kind of bud, one which is surrounded by shoots which can grow on around it, as opposed to the terminal bud which is surrounded by other flower buds. The first crown buds on a chrysanthemum are the first flower buds to appear after one stopping (*centre*). The second crown buds are those that result from a second stopping (*right*). *See also* Break; Corona; Cutting; Stopping.

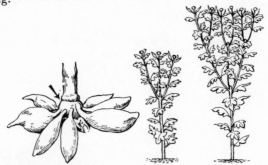

CRUCIFER. Any member of the mustard family, *Cruciferae*, which includes wallflowers, stocks, aubrieta, arabis, alyssum, sweet rocket, water cress and brassicas. The name refers to the cross-like arrangement of the four petals, which are usually equal in size though sometimes there are two large and two small petals. There are other plants with four petals, but the combination of these with four sepals and six (rarely four) stamens makes crucifers readily distinguishable from other plants. The Siberian wallflower is illustrated.

CUCKOO-SPIT. *See* Spit.

CULTIVAR. *See* Genus; Variety.

CUP. A name given to the corona of narcissi when it is shorter than the length of the perianth segments. In large-cupped narcissi (Division II of the R.H.S. Daffodil Classification) the cup is more than one-third the length of the perianth segments (*right*); in small-cupped (Division III), less than one-third (*left*). Some large-cups look almost like trumpet narcissi, but this term should be reserved for those in which the corona is as long or longer than the perianth segments (Division I). *See also* Corona; Trumpet.

CUTTING. A cutting is a portion of leaf, stem or root separated from a plant and treated in such a way that it produces roots and eventually grows into a new plant. It differs from a division in that the latter will already have some roots; though the phrase  'Irishman's cutting' is sometimes used to denote shoots, pulled from the crown or rootstock of a plant, which have already made roots. Many plants may each be increased by various different types of cutting, especially where stem cuttings are used, when the degree of maturity of the shoot determines the kind of cutting and the time to take it. Illustrated, *left to right*, are a shrubby stem cutting; a leaf-bud cutting of a short piece of stem; and a leaf cutting. *See also* Crown; Division; Eye; Heel; Joint; Piping; Strike.

CYME. A term covering a number of types of flower-head, in all of which the growing points end in a flower and further flowers  are carried on a succession of side branches. Thus the central flowers open first and the flower-head is commonly dome-shaped, or may be flat-topped. *Chlora perfoliata*, a common plant of chalk downs, is illustrated (*left*). One curious form of cyme, known as a scorpioid, is a unilateral one often found in the family Boraginaceae, and more easy to illustrate than describe: *Myosotis palustris* (water forget-me not) is shown (*right*).

DAMPING. Damping down is the operation of moistening paths and stagings in a greenhouse—not usually the plants themselves—to maintain air humidity.

Damping off is a name covering various fungus diseases affecting seedlings, which causes them to rot near soil level, and is encouraged by overcrowding, excess humidity, poor drainage, and soggy or unsterilised soil. A chemical called Cheshunt Compound will control the disease.

DECIDUOUS. Losing leaves annually, usually in the winter; mainly referring to trees. The opposite to Evergreen.

DECUSSATE. *See* Opposite.

DENTATE. *See* Toothed.

DIBBER, DIBBLE. A tool used for making holes in soil into which seeds, seedlings or cuttings may be inserted. Their size will vary according to the size of the seed or plant, from something resembling an ordinary pencil, or pieces of dowel with a rounded

end (*left*), to those the size of a spade-handle. An old handle can be converted or dibbers with steel tips can be bought (*right*). It is better to have a rounded end rather than a pointed one. Dibble is an alternative spelling, and also the verb describing the use of the tool. It is often quicker to dibble in seedlings than to use a trowel. *See also* Pricking Out.

DIGGING. *See* Ridging; Spit; Trenching.

DIGITATE. *See* Palmate.

DIOECIOUS, MONOECIOUS. When a plant is described as dioecious it means that the male and female flowers are carried on distinct plants, as in the sea buckthorn (*left*), skimmias, pernettyas and some hollies. The sea buckthorn flowers are shown

enlarged (M, male; F, female): the flowers of most dioecious plants are small. When such plants are prized for their fruits it is necessary to plant a male among several females to ensure a set of berries. In a monoecious plant the male and female flowers are carried separately but on the same plant, as in the hazel (*right*); the catkins contain the male flowers, while the females are in small bud-like spikes.

DISBUDDING. The removal of surplus buds or shoots concentrates the efforts of the stem concerned into the one bud left, forcing it to develop to its fullest extent. Disbudding is essential with exhibition roses, carnations and chrysanthemums. In the first two cases surplus buds are removed around the chosen one; with chrysanthemums it is more often surplus shoots around
the bud that are removed. Usually the bud chosen to flower is the terminal one, but if for some reason this bud produces excessively large or full flowers a side bud may be chosen. Disbudding should normally be carried out at the earliest possible moment. *See also* Take; Terminal.

DISK. *See* Composite.

DIVISION. The easiest way of increasing clump-forming plants is to cut, pull or tease the roots apart. With vigorous herbaceous plants it is usually best to retain only the outer growths and to discard the old, worn-out centre (*right*). Some herbaceous plants may need the leverage of two garden forks to pull apart the tough roots (*left*). With fragile pot plants, like the African violet, which make several crowns, division needs the careful use of a sharp knife.

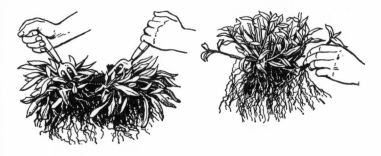

DOT PLANT. A tall plant used, especially in bedding schemes, in a groundwork of lower plants, to give contrast and height. Any plant can be so used; among those favoured in formal bedding are variegated abutilons, *Eucalyptus globulus*, cannas, kochias (illustrated) and standard fuchsias and pelargoniums.

DOUBLE, SEMI-DOUBLE. Wild plants occasionally produce flowers with more than the normal number of petals, and from these have been bred many of our fully double garden flowers, such as hybrid tea roses, peonies and camellias, in which the whole flower is filled with petals. A single and double hollyhock are illustrated (*left*). In these flowers the stamens and pistils are often more or less replaced by the petals. A double flower may be

designated botanically by the words flore pleno or their abbreviation fl. pl., or sometimes by the word plena or pleniflora alone. Where a flower has more than the usual number of petals, but is not fully double, it is called semi-double. Many floribunda roses are of this type (*right*), and such flowers usually have a full complement of stamens and pistil.

DRAWN. Plants grown in the dark, or crowded together, will become tall and spindly, which the gardener describes as drawn. Plants recover from this condition with difficulty, and a drawn seedling is never the same again; for this reason early thinning and pricking off, and placing seedlings in maximum light, are necessary. A drawn tomato seedling is shown (*left*) with a healthy one of the same age (*right*). The word drawing is used in connection with making drills with a hoe, *for which see on facing page.*

DRILL. A narrow furrow made in soil, usually with the corner of some kind of hoe, for seed sowing or occasionally for the reception of seedlings. The act of making a drill is often called drawing a drill or drilling. Most seeds only need a drill $\frac{1}{4}$ to $\frac{1}{2}$ in. deep, though peas, beans and other large seeds must be buried more deeply. After sowing, the seeds are covered by drawing the displaced soil back into the drill.

DRUPE. A fruit comprising an outer skin, a fleshy layer, and a

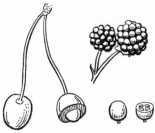

hard 'stone' protecting the seed proper. Cherries and plums (*left*) are simple drupes. Compound drupes include those of raspberry and blackberry (*centre*), in which the flesh-coated seeds are grouped together, and those of holly (*right*) and elder, in which each berry contains several seeds or nuts. *See also* Berry; Stone.

EARTHING UP. To earth up is to draw soil towards or around plants. This is done for several reasons. With leeks and celery gradual earthing up is essential to blanch the stems and make them palatable. The sketches show celery at planting time and when

mature and fully earthed up. Potatoes are habitually earthed up, again gradually, to avoid greening of the tubers. Earthing up may also be necessary with tall brassicas—broccoli, cauliflowers, kales—to prevent windrock.

EMASCULATION. The removal of the anthers of a flower to prevent it from becoming fertilised with its own pollen. This is usually essential when carrying out cross-fertilisation in breeding programmes, and may sometimes have to be done before the bud opens. *See also* Fertilisation.

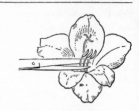

ENTIRE. A botanical term applied to leaves with completely smooth, unindented margins, whatever the general shape of the leaf.

EPIPHYTE. A plant which grows upon another without being in any way a parasite; it obtains lodging but not food from its 'host'. Many orchids and bromeliads are epiphytic, obtaining their nourishment partly from the moist air and partly from decaying

leaves, etc., which collect among the roots. (Illustrated is *Angraecum eburneum.*) Many such plants have aerial roots specially adapted to obtain atmospheric moisture under such conditions, and in cultivation it is beneficial to try to imitate natural growth habits, though by no means essential. It is not usual to include under this definition plants such as ivies and philodendrons which climb up trees, clinging with aerial roots, but with their main feeding roots in the ground. *See also* Aerial Root.

ERICACEOUS. Any plant belonging to the *Ericaceae*, or heather family, which includes erica, calluna, arbutus, kalmia, pieris and rhododendron, to name but a few. Though rhododendrons and azaleas usually have open, trumpet-shaped flowers (*left*), many ericaceous plants have small bell-shaped ones, like pieris (*right*). Kalmia has a more oddly shaped flower (*centre*). Most of the Ericaceae are calcifuge plants, insisting on acid, peaty soils with a pH of 6·5 or less. *See also* Calcicole; Calcifuge.

ESPALIER. A system of horizontal wires for training fruit trees, either supported by horizontal posts or on a wall. The word also refers to trees so trained, which have a vertical main trunk from

which side branches are trained horizontally along the wires to right and left, about 15 in. apart. In more spacious days espaliers with ten or twenty tiers might be trained on a wall; nowadays, most gardeners content themselves with three or four. In effect each branch is a cordon, and is treated as such. *See also* Spur.

EVERLASTING. Though slightly misleading, this word is applied to certain flowers with papery or chaffy petals or bracts which last a very long time, especially if carefully dried. Many are composites, including the one most commonly called 'everlasting', helichrysum (*top left*), and ammobium, anaphalis, helipterum and xeranthemum. The sea lavenders (*below left*)—several species of statice or more properly limonium—the globe amaranth, gomphrena, and the shell flower, molucella (*right*), are others. To dry these they are best cut before fully open and hung in small bunches in a cool, airy, shaded place. Some garden and wild flowers which may be dried in a similar way include teasels, globe thistles, love-lies-bleeding, *Achillea filipendulina*, grasses, and the seed pods of honesty and physalis or Chinese lantern. The French word immortelle is also sometimes used for such flowers.

EYE. There are several horticultural meanings of 'eye'. It usually indicates a bud, like the growth buds on a potato (*below, left*) or dahlia tuber; also the single bud on a short piece of stem used as a cutting for grape vines (*below, right*).

Another meaning refers to the centre of a flower when it is differently coloured to the rest, as in many pinks (*above, left*).

Primroses are described as pin-eyed (*above, centre*) or thrum-eyed (*above, right*) according to whether the stigma or stamens are visible at the top of the corolla tube. The latter term derives from the word 'thrum', meaning a tassel or piece of loose yarn on cloth, and refers to the appearance of the anthers bunched together.

F.1. The first generation from a cross. *See* Hybrid; Hybrid Vigour.

F.2. The second generation from a cross.

FAIRY RING. Most fungi of toadstool shape tend to grow in rings as the mycelium, or 'spawn', grows outwards from its point of origin. One, *Marasmius oreades* (illustrated), is so often found in rings that it is called the Fairy Ring Mushroom, and is frequently troublesome on lawns and sports greens, much more so than other kinds. The fungus absorbs all the food within the soil it occupies, so that it can only grow outwards; in extreme cases the dead mycelium so fills up the soil that no moisture can be absorbed and the grass above dies, leaving the bare ring which not long ago was attributed to dancing fairies. Often the grass on either side of the ring is more vigorous and of a deeper green—the ring is often visible for this reason when no fungi can be seen above ground. On the outside of the ring this is due to the release of ammonia by the living fungus, and within it is due to the release of nitrogenous matter as the dead mycelium decays. Some fungi do not send up the toadstools, which are technically fruit-bodies and shed the

reproductive spores, for many years. Huge rings can be found, as on the South Downs, which are several centuries old. On the lawn, they can be dealt with by pricking and then watering with a solution of sulphate of iron, 4 oz. in a gallon of water, or in extreme cases by digging out the infected soil and replacing it. *See also* Fungus.

FALCATE. Sickle-shaped.

FALL. *See* Beard.

FAMILY. *See*   enus.

FAN. A self-explanatory word referring to a shape of trained tree on walls, mainly used with peaches, apricots and nectarines, though equally applicable to plums and cherries. Apples and pears lend themselves more to training as cordons and espaliers, but could be trained as fans. In a fan the branches are trained

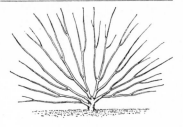

straight, radiating if possible from the top of a central leg, which can be 6 or 12 in. tall in a dwarf fan or as long as 6 ft. with a standard fan.

FARINA. Literally farina means flour or meal, and it is applied botanically to the powdery coating on the stems, leaves and occasionally flowers of certain plants, notably primulas, which is a form of protection similar to the waxy 'bloom' on plums, leaves of

some succulents, and so on. This meal is usually white but sometimes bluish or yellowish, and can add to the beauty of the plant. The specific name of *Primula farinosa*, the bird's-eye primrose (*left*), describes its dusty appearance. Pulverulent, which literally means dusty, is also used in specific names to describe mealy plants, such as *Primula pulverulenta*. Some garden auriculas are called Dusty Millers for the same reason. The appearance of farina reaches the height of oddity in the show auricula, in some variety of which the petals have a central zone of mealy 'paste' and an outer zone of lighter meal (*right*); the leaves are usually mealy too.

FASCIATION. A freak condition in which, typically, the stem of a plant becomes flat and strap-shaped, giving the impression of several stems fused together, and the flower at its end may also develop abnormally in one place (*left, overleaf*), or a great number of flowers be produced (*right*). It is common in cacti and ferns, where fasciated plants are called cristates and are prized by collectors. Many garden plants can be affected, including lupins, lilies, delphiniums, primulas, chrysanthemums, gaillardias, etc. Sometimes only one stem of a plant is affected and the plant will seldom be fasciated the following year. There is nothing to be done about it. The cause is obscure, but seems to be initially due to damage to

37

the microscopic growing tip of
the shoot; and the occurence
of fasciation varies from year
to year, sometimes being very
frequent. It has been sug-
gested that mild, warm
weather or other reason for
unusually rapid growth may
encourage it. Records show,
incidentally, that fasciation
was frequent long before atom
bombs were thought of. *See
also* Cristate.

FASTIGIATE. This term, from a Latin word meaning the top
of a gable, indicates a plant of erect habit, and is usually applied to

forms of trees and shrubs which
normally have spreading branches,
but in these special varieties have
upright branches. Examples include
the Lombardy poplar (illustrated,
with normal type of *Populus nigra*);
the upright cherry Amanogawa, a
form of *Prunus serrulata*; the Dawyck
beech, a variety of the common
beech; and there are quite a number
of others. They are valuable as
features in garden design, and also
where space is limited.

FEATHERED, FLAKED, FLAMED. Fanciers use special
words to describe the markings on their flowers. Feathered is

primarily applied to a type of 'broken' tulip, but also to other
flowers with similar markings, such as crocuses, in which a fine

pencilling in a different colour to the groundwork extends mainly around the edges of the petals (*centre*). A flamed tulip (*left*) has, in addition to the feathering, a band of solid colour up the centre of the petal, which branches and joins the feathering. Flaked is most often applied to carnations (*right*); there is a class of carnation known as 'flakes' but few now exist and flaking is also a characteristic of the less regularly marked 'fancies'. In all these carnation types streaks and bands of deeper colour overlay a different ground, white in the true flake. The 'bizarre' carnation is flaked in two or more colours on a differently coloured ground. *See also* Maiden; Virus.

FERN. A member of the group known as Filices: non-flowering, rather primitive perennial plants whose green parts are referred to as fronds and which multiply by spores, not seeds. *See also* Frond; Spore.

FERTILISATION. Ferti-
lisation consists in the union
of two cells of opposite sex to
produce a new individual;
in the case of plants a seed is
first produced which is capable, in the right conditions,
of growing into a new adult.
This is the result of a pollen
grain (p, p, p on diagrammatic section, *left*) growing

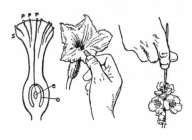

down the female stigma (s) until it fuses with the embryo sac (e) in the ovule (o). In many plants wind or insects transmit the pollen, but the gardener may have to do this artificially if he wishes to ensure the production of seed or fruit. In the case of peaches under glass a camel-hair brush (*right*) or rabbit's tail tied to a stick may be used. A brush is also used on flowers when the breeder is carrying out specific crosses. With melons and, to a lesser extent, marrows, but not greenhouse cucumbers (which taste bitter if they set seed)—a male flower can be picked off and the pollen applied to the female flower direct from the stamens (*centre*). *See also* Emasculation; Hybrid; Parthenocarpic; Stigma.

FILAMENT. *See* Anther.

FLAKED, FLAMED. *See* Feathered.

FLORE PLENO (Fl. Pl.) *See* Double.

FORCING. When plants are hurried into growth at an unnatural time by artificial means this is described as forcing. Gentle heat is the usual accelerator, and is applied in particular to spring bulbs (after a period in cool conditions—*see* Plunge) and to early-flowering shrubs, kept most of the year in cool conditions in pots. Lilies-of-the-valley retarded in cold conditions will then respond rapidly to heat. Some vegetables force better in darkness, notably seakale and chicory, which need blanching in any case, and rhubarb; these can be forced under the greenhouse staging or in a warm shed. *See also* Vernalisation.

FORM. *See* Strain.

FRAME. A garden frame is a low structure which can be covered with glazed lights, using glass, glass substitute or plastic film. Frames are used to hasten seed germination and the rooting of cuttings, to obtain certain crops such as early salads when they could not be grown outside, to harden off plants such as half-hardy annuals raised in the greenhouse which are to be planted outside, and to protect slightly tender subjects in winter. The standard old-fashioned garden frames had lights 6 by 4 ft. or 3 by 4 ft. with several sash bars (*left*), but today, especially in commercial use, the Dutch frame (*centre*), taking a light of a single pane 62 by 25 in., is in much greater use, as it is easier to handle and transmits far more light. Some modern frames employ metal frameworks (*right*), though most are still of wood. The sides can be of wood or brick or, for a temporary frame, of turves. A propagating frame is usually small and must be tight-fitting to ensure the close atmosphere necessary for the rooting of cuttings. It is commonly placed inside a greenhouse over a source of heat. Ordinary frames can, of course, be heated, the most convenient method being soil-warming cables. *See also* Bottom Heat; Hardening Off.

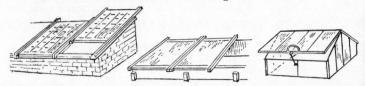

FROND. A frond is the technical term for the leaf of a fern, and varies in shape as much as leaves of higher plants. On the underside are carried the sporangia, which contain the spores, equivalent to seeds. These are grouped together in distinctively shaped masses

called the sori (singular sorus).
These only appear at certain
times and are occasionally mis-
taken by the uninitiated for
symptoms of a fungus infection. These sori are normally
brownish and may be circular,
arranged in lines, or in other
patterns. Illustrated are phyl-
litis (*left*), adiantum (*centre,
above*), and one leaflet or pinna
of dryopteris (*centre, below*).
S, s indicate sori. In a few
ferns the sori are carried on fronds of different shape to the ordinary
sterile ones, or, as in botrychium (*right*), on a separate stem to the
frond. The Royal Fern, *Osmunda regalis*, is an impressive example
of this, and is sometimes called Flowering Fern for this reason.
See also Pinna; Spore.

FRUTICOSE. *See* Shrub.

FUNGUS. The fungi (plural of fungus) are one of the most
important divisions of the vegetable kingdom. Though differing
greatly in size, appearance and habits, they all lack chlorophyll, the
green colouring matter of ordinary plants, and being thus unable
to produce their food from simple chemicals via the sun's energy

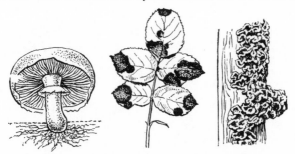

they must obtain food supplies either from living plants or animals,
when they are parasites, or from decaying matter, when they are
saprophytes, like most mushrooms and toadstools. The mushroom
(*left*) is only the reproductive organ or 'fruit-body' of the fungus,
producing the microscopic spores which are the equivalent of
seeds. The fungus proper is a tangle of thread-like growth known

as the mycelium, as anyone who has grown mushrooms will know: the 'spawn' used to start a mushroom bed is a compact piece of this mycelium.

Many fungi are parasites which cause a variety of plant diseases, such as scab, mildew, black spot (*centre*), etc. Some of these fungi are microscopic, but others produce large fruit-bodies, like the silver leaf fungus after it has killed its host (*right*). However, many fungi are beneficial, for they help to break down dead plant and animal matter and release the valuable chemical plant foods which they contain. *See also* Fairy Ring; Parasite; Saprophyte; Spore; Symbiosis; Witch's Broom.

FUNNELFORM. A self-explanatory term used in describing certain flowers (*Ipomaea tricolor*, the morning glory, is illustrated), or other structures. The Latin equivalent infundibuliformis is sometimes seen as a descriptive specific name.

GALL. Galls are abnormal outgrowths on plants, caused most frequently by insects, which lay eggs in the leaf, stem, flower or roots, and also by eelworms, bacteria and fungi. Exactly how they arise is uncertain; the organism responsible irritates the plant tissue, in the case of the insects probably by a liquid secretion, and the plant reacts by abnormal growth. It is rather mysterious

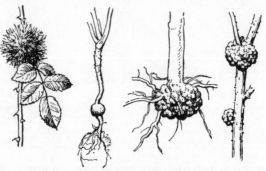

how different insects can affect the same plant in entirely distinct ways, each kind of gall being clearly recognisable.

Most of the insect galls—such as oak apples, the hairy 'robin's pincushion' (*left*) on roses, and the little red knobs on willow leaves, to mention some familiar ones—are virtually harmless, but the gall weevil of cabbage roots (*left, centre*) sometimes plagues the gardener. Azalea gall is one caused by a fungus. Crown and leafy galls are caused by bacteria, and are apparently wound infections.

On fruit trees crown galls form round, hard, woody swellings (*right, centre*, on a rootstock) which are seldom harmful, but on plants like dahlias, chrysanthemums, gladioli, etc., the large, soft swelling weakens the host, and gall, plant and all are best consigned to the fire. Despite their name crown galls can be formed on the upper parts of a plant, as they often are on raspberries (*right*). Leafy galls are similar but consist of a great number of short, distorted shoots.

GENE. *See* Chromosome.

GENUS.

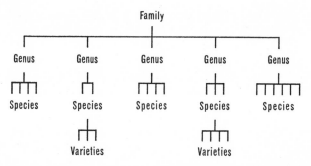

A genus (plural genera) is a classificatory term, indicating a group of plants (or, of course, animals)—occasionally only one— which are similar in structure and may be supposed to have evolved from a common ancestor. The members of a genus are known as species (singular and plural) and each species, though sometimes slightly variable in detail, persistently breeds true in its main characters. The generic and specific names combined provide an international name for the plant, e.g., the wallflower is *Cheiranthus* (generic) *cheiri* (specific). Genera are grouped into families (sometimes called Natural Orders) in which certain characters are constant or at least readily to be differentiated from those of other families; thus the family *Cruciferae* to which *Cheiranthus* belongs have four sepals, four petals, six stamens—two being shorter or rarely wanting—a single style and two-celled solitary ovary. Garden varieties, which are officially known as cultivars, are derived from individual species by selection or by cross-breeding. Natural varieties also occur. Varieties, though often very different in colouring and even form, are botanically similar to the species or type. The diagram illustrates the principle of classification.

The characters used for defining plant families and genera are almost exclusively those of the flower, fruit and seed; leaves and habit may vary tremendously within a single genus. Often genera of one family, and even species of one genus, look superficially different, but close examination of the floral characters reveals the relationship. *See also* Variety.

GERMINATION. The earliest stage in the development of a seed; its sprouting. *See also* Cotyledon; Pricking Out.

GLABROUS. Glabrous should simply mean 'not hairy', but it is sometimes loosely, and wrongly, used in the more positive sense of 'smooth'. A glabrous leaf can be rough or irregular, but a smooth one cannot.

GLAND. Plant glands are organs which are presumed to secrete unwanted substances such as resins and ethereal oils. They consist of small vesicles which may be embedded in, on or slightly protruding from the surface of any part of a plant—stem, leaf, bract, flower parts or fruit. The sugar-secreting nectaries of flowers are a kind of gland and nectaries are sometimes found outside the flowers, as on the leaves of cherries and of laurel. When the glands are carried on a thin stalk they are known as glandular hairs; sometimes they are carried on relatively very thick stalks, as in *Impatiens glandulifera* (*centre*). Some of the most interesting and highly developed glandular hairs are those which sting, like those of the nettle (*right*, much magnified) and those of insectivorous plants, as in the sundew (Drosera, *left*), which are not only sticky to hold, and later digest, insects but are sensitive to touch and bend over to trap the prey as shown.

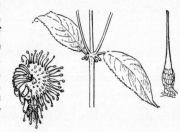

GLAUCOUS. Bluish grey, or covered with a bluish 'bloom' like a plum.

GRAFTING. A graft is a union between two plants, which can occur in natural conditions (as when two branches rub into each other and finally, as they expand, grow together), but is normally an artificial procedure. It depends for its success on the ability of wounded plant tissue, under the right circumstances, to produce a callus; when wounded tissues are placed together it is the calluses that unite and eventually enable the two plants to grow as one. Only plants which are quite closely related can be grafted. The principle is widely used to propagate plants which are either difficult or relatively slow to raise from cuttings, or which are unsatisfactory on their own roots, or which cannot be raised true from seed—notably fruit trees. Many different methods have been developed according to the plants involved and the parts of the plant used; but in all cases the part of the plant which provides the roots is known as the stock, while the top part, selected for its fruit or flower, is called the scion.

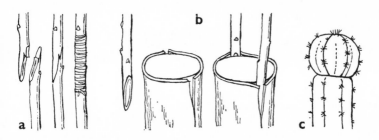

Perhaps the most commonly used method of grafting is the whip and tongue, used with young fruit and ornamental trees. The principle is shown in the three sketches a. Note the binding together of stock and scion to ensure rigidity; this is done with almost all kinds of graft and the junction is then covered with grafting wax or similar material to prevent drying out.

As a contrast, the rind graft is used on old stocks, as in rejuvenating old fruit trees; the stock is much bigger than the scion, and several scions can sometimes be inserted round the same stock—see sketches b. Budding, the main method of increasing roses, is another form of grafting.

Perhaps the simplest plants to graft are cacti; here it is only necessary to cut the two plants concerned to provide corresponding flat surfaces (sketch c) and to fix these in place with ties or by pinning with a cactus spine. *See also* Budding; Callus; Chimaera; Inarching; Scion; Standard; Stub; Sucker.

GREEN MANURING. *See* Nodule.

HAIRY. Any degree of hairiness—the opposite of glabrous—can be denoted by a variety of words, which are often, however, used rather loosely. Hairy or hirsute indicates rather coarse, dense hairs. Hispid or bristly denotes stiffer dense hairs, and setose very stiff, erect, straight hairs. Pilose means with long, sparse hairs; hoary or canescent with dense, short, whitish hairs, too small to be seen individually but making the plant look frosted. Woolly, cottony and felted, each of which can also be called tomentose, are self-explanatory, as is downy or pubescent, while puberulent means slightly downy and villous covered with long, weak hairs or down. Many of these words are used in specific names, as hirsutus, hispidus, setosus, pilosus, canescens, tomentosus, villosus and pubescens. Illustrated are a bristly leaf of *Echium plantagineum* (*left*) and a felted one of *Kalanchoë tomentosa* (*right*).

The hairs themselves can be variously shaped—plumose or feathery, stellate or star-shaped, and scaly when they form little

circular discs with a central pillar, though it usually needs close examination to see these formations. Hairs of any kind, presumably, have as function the protection of the leaf or stem surface against excessive light or heat: alpines, some cacti and many other succulents are often protected in this way. *See also* Ciliate.

HARDENING OFF. Plants often start life in much warmer conditions than are needed when they are adult, and they have to be gradually adjusted to the lower temperatures; this is called hardening off. If this is done too quickly a severe and even fatal check may be given. This is especially so with plants raised in the warm greenhouse early in the year which are destined to flower outside. The first stage may be to remove seedlings from a propagator into the main greenhouse; then the plants are moved to the coolest part of the house, and later to a cold frame. Here exposure to the outside air is steadily increased, though protection is given in bad weather or when frost threatens. Any stoppage of growth, or blueing or yellowing of foliage, indicates that the plants have been subjected to cold too quickly. *See also* Frame.

HARDY. A vague term which basically means that a plant so called will be capable of growing outside without protection all the year round. Obviously, however, some plants may be hardy in mild Cornwall and not hardy on the cold east coast; local climates vary too, while the degree of local shelter and even the kind of soil, as well as physiological factors, also affect hardiness. *See also* Tender.

HEEL. If a cutting is prepared by pulling a side-shoot away from the main shoot, rather than cutting it, a small strip of bark and wood from the main shoot is dragged away with it. This is called a heel and any cutting so prepared is a heel cutting. It is best to trim the ragged edges back neatly, but not to remove the heel because in some cases (though not all) cuttings with a heel strike more readily. *See also* Cutting.

HEELING IN. A term used for temporary planting, usually before putting plants in their permanent positions. Shrubs, trees and herbaceous plants may arrive from the nursery, or be in process of transfer from another garden, before their permanent site is ready, or when the weather is too wet or cold to allow planting them in their final places. In such cases a trench is dug in any convenient place—avoiding a position likely to become waterlogged—and the plant roots are placed in this close together, covered with soil and made firm with the foot. Plants can remain heeled in like this for several weeks, especially in winter months

when they are more or less dormant. Heeling in is also often used for spring bulbs which must be moved to make room for bedding plants but which have not finished their growth. If heeled in close together the bulbs will have a chance of ripening fully.

HERBACEOUS. The opposite of woody or shrubby; usually applied to plants the top growth of which dies down each year.

HERMAPHRODITE. A flower with both sexes together.

HISPID, HOARY. *See* Hairy.

HOLLOW-TINE FORK. *See* Tine.

HORMONE. Certain organic chemicals in plants control various aspects of growth. Synthetic materials based upon these, which are loosely called hormones, have been developed to give the gardener exterior control of plant growth: they will assist in forming roots, setting fruits, preventing fruit drop, retarding growth and killing broad-leaved weeds.

HOSE-IN-HOSE. A floral abnormality akin to doubling, in which one perfect flower is carried within another, sometimes  sufficiently separate to look as if it has grown from the lower one. It particularly affects the primula family (illustrated), while such duplex mimulus, rhododendrons and azaleas are also found. Many of these mutations are very attractive; the Elizabethans used to prize such flowers and there are cultivated today a considerable number of named varieties of hose-in-hose primroses and polyanthus, in particular.

HOTBED. *See* Bottom Heat.

HUMUS. One of the most important factors in gardening and agriculture, humus is, to quote the Oxford Dictionary, 'the dark brown or black substance resulting from the slow decomposition of organic matter'; and the scientist would agree with this, though the chemical structure of humus has defied research. The gardener uses the word more loosely to include organic matter which may not be completely decayed. Completely decayed humus is colloidal: that is, it is a jelly-like substance which coats the soil particles, swelling when wet and shrinking when dry. This is one of its important properties, which improves the texture of the soil by

48

making it spongy and water-retaining without spoiling its crumb structure or letting it become waterlogged. In the humus multiply the bacteria which break down the complex materials of dead plant and animal tissue into the simpler chemicals which plants absorb as food.

Humus disappears steadily in any given soil as the bacteria work in it, and any kind of cultivation greatly hastens its destruction. For this reason, humus - providing materials must be constantly added to soil in proportion to the intensity of cultivation. Humus may be supplied by animal manures, vegetable refuse, leaf-mould, seaweed, peat, spent hops, straw and also by animal residues such as shoddy, offal and fish waste. Most of these substances, except peat, hops and shoddy, should be rotted down before working them into the soil, and the compost heap is the best place for this. The sketch shows fresh manure being forked over coarse vegetable rubbish as the foundation of a heap. Organic fertilisers such as bonemeal and hoof and horn meal also supply humus in a small degree, unlike inorganic materials. The provision of humus and the consequent improvement of soil texture must not be confused with the food value of any organic material: thus animal manure is highly nutritious to plants and peat practically not at all, but both are soil improvers.

HYBRID. To the botanist a hybrid is the result of cross-fertilisation between two species of plant or animal, but to the gardener the term is more loosely applied to the results of crossing between varieties. A very few hybrids are true-breeding, but in most cases they are not, and a few are sterile. A primary hybrid—the result of a cross between two species—will usually show some of the characteristics of both parents, and a batch of primary hybrids between the same two parents will usually be similar, if not identical. Once one starts to use plants of hybrid origin as parents, however, the offspring usually become more and more variable, due to the innumerable recombinations of character-carrying genes which can occur. The botanist indicates a hybrid by the

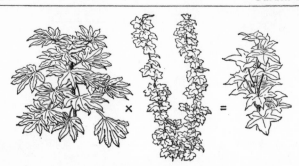

sign × (e.g., *Erica* × *veitchii* is a cross between *E. arborea* and *E. lusitanica*). A number of cases of intergeneric hybrids are known, i.e., the results of crossing plants of two distinct genera. One of these is the foliage plant *Fatshedera lizei* (*right*), result of crossing the large-leaved, erect *Fatsia japonica* (*left*) with the climbing *Hedera hibernica*, the Irish ivy (*centre*). The offspring is an upright plant with ivy-like leaves.

Intergeneric hybrids are common among orchids, where three or even four genera may have been used as grandparents and parents. Such hybrids are commonly given composite names like *Brassolaeliocattleya*—hybrids between *Brassavola*, *Laelia* and *Cattleya*. *See also* Chromosome; Emasculation; Fertilisation.

HYBRID VIGOUR. If two different, selected varieties of a plant are crossed, the offspring will often have what is called hybrid vigour, shown in larger size or improved cropping capacity. This principle has been applied to sweet corn and tomatoes on a commercial scale, and also to certain flowers such as petunias. The diagram (reproduced by the kind permission of the John Innes

Institute) shows the increased vigour of sweet corn in the F1 generation (as the first offspring of a cross are called) after crossing the two pure parent strains P1 and P2. The diagram also shows

how the vigour declines in the subsequent generations F2, F3, etc., if the hybrids are cross-pollinated, and this means that the original cross has to be made each year to produce a new batch of F1 seed. It is therefore of little use to save seeds from an F1 or hybrid vigour variety. One should add that not all plants will produce hybrid vigour.

HYGROMETER. An instrument which measures humidity.

IMBRICATE. This term is directly derived from a Latin word which simply means overlapping, and usually refers to leaves, scales or bracts laid closely one on the other. Tree buds are often covered with imbricate scales (*left*). The word is sometimes used as a specific name: thus the Monkey-puzzle was originally called *Araucaria imbricata* (now it is *A. araucana*) because of the closely overlapping leaves (*right*).

IMMORTELLE. *See* Everlasting.

INARCHING. A method of grafting sometimes more descriptively known as grafting by approach. In this technique the scion continues to grow on its own roots until the union with the stock is made. This means that the plant providing the scion is grown in a pot, and sometimes the stock plant also. The plants are arranged so that the stems are alongside (a), and in the simplest method a sliver of bark and wood about 2 in. long is taken off each, on the facing sides (b). Other methods include the use of 'tongues' (c) and 'inlays'. The two cut surfaces are then bound together with raffia (d) and the whole area covered with grafting wax, as in other methods of grafting. When the two cut surfaces have made a good union the scion is cut just below the point of union and the

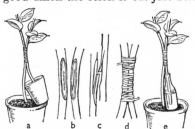

upper part of the stock is likewise removed. Where the scion plant cannot conveniently be brought to the stock the bottle graft may be used, in which the base of the scion is kept in water until union is made (e). *See also* Grafting.

51

INCURVED, INCURVING. Literally meaning curving inwards, incurving is a word applied mainly to a group of chrysanthemums in which the florets turn loosely upwards and inwards. Incurved refers to the group in which the florets curve very closely and tightly together, the result being a compact globular flower. The opposite of Recurved, *which see.*

INFLORESCENCE. A general term which covers the flowering part of a plant, whatever the size of the individual flower or the number of flowers that are grouped together. The examples illustrated (not to scale) are (*left*) eschscholzia, a single flower on a single

stem; (*centre*) calendula, a composite inflorescence made up of numerous florets in an involucre; and (*right*) Lysimachia vulgaris, one of the many types of branching flowerhead, in this case a panicle. *See also* Cyme; Panicle; Raceme; Spike; Truss; Umbel.

INTERNODE. *See* Joint.

INVOLUCRE. A collection of bracts, usually in a whorl, at or just below the base of an inflorescence, the latter usually being a condensed or compound flower-head so that the involucre forms a structure more or less like a calyx. The involucre is a characteristic structure of the daisy family, *Compositae*; illustrated (*left*) is the cardoon, which has a rather exaggerated involucre. It is usually found in the teasel and scabious family, *Dipsacaceae*, and some-

times in the *Umbelliferae*, as in the sea holly and astrantia (*centre*). It is also found in other families, as for instance in the kidney vetch, anthyllis (*right*) of the pea family, *Leguminosae. See also* Bract; Composite; Umbellifer.

IRISHMAN'S CUTTING. *See* Cutting.

IRREGULAR. Flowers are said to be irregular when some of one series of parts (e.g. petals) differ from others. The antirrhinum and salvia are examples (*see under* Corolla and Lip for illustrations).

JOINT. The points on an adult plant stem at which leaves or leaf buds appear are known as joints or nodes. These are sometimes pronounced, as in grasses and bamboos (*left*) and other plants with hollow or pithy stems, which are usually closed internally at the  nodes. Plants may be referred to as short- or long-jointed, as the case may be, and those in which the joints or nodes are pronounced are sometimes called articulate. The latter term is sometimes used as a specific name, as in the Candle Plant, *Kleinia articulata* (*centre*), where the stems, which root readily, are literally jointed and often break at these points. In this case the jointing is not associated with leaf formation.

Growth buds are often found at each joint and the cambium layer at this point is more capable of producing adventitious roots or buds than elsewhere on the stem; hence most cuttings should be trimmed just below a joint; as in the carnation (*right*). In a few cases, e.g. clematis, cuttings are best taken between the joints, and these are called internodal cuttings. *See also* Adventitious; Cutting.

KEEL. *See* Leguminous.

KNOT. *See* Parterre.

LABIATE. *See* Lip.

LACINIATE. Cut into narrow and usually irregular segments; a botanical term usually applied to leaves that are lobed in this way, but also to petals, when the narrow segments look like a fringe, as in

Dianthus superbus (*left*). The word is sometimes Latinised as a specific or varietal name, and the other sketches show (*centre*), leaflets of *Rhus typhina laciniata* with (*right*) the normal form of the species.

53

LANCEOLATE. Literally, lance-shaped: a botanical term usually applied to leaves which are a good deal longer than wide and taper to both ends. It is often seen as a specific name, as in *Tricuspidaria lanceolata* (illustrated).

LATERAL, LEADER. Laterals are, literally, side-shoots of any kind, while the leader is the shoot which terminates a branch and will continue, if left, to extend it in the same general direction. The central leader is the vertical continuation of the trunk. These terms are primarily used in explaining fruit tree pruning, for on a fruit tree the laterals are usually the fruit-producers: if left uncut they produce fruit buds relatively quickly. Fruit tree laterals are sometimes described as maiden or one-year, two-year, and three-year laterals, according to their age, such definition being essential when pruning trees.

The sketch also shows a replacement leader which will eventually take the place of the existing branch system shown. These terms can, of course, also be applied to shrubs and trees of all kinds. *See also* Pruning.

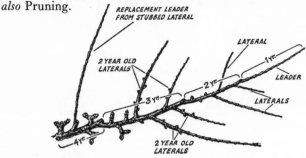

LATEX. Milky sap.

LAYERING. A method of propagation in which a shoot is made to form roots while still attached to the parent plant. A number of plants do this naturally, including the bramble family. The shoot being rooted, and the same shoot when it has formed roots and been cut from the parent, is referred to as a layer. When making a layer the stem is either slit to form a 'tongue', or notched or ringed, or it is twisted and bent in one place, in order to check the flow of sap at the point of contact between stem and soil. Where any kind of cut is made this should be below a bud or node. The tongue or bend is buried in the soil, which can with advantage contain gritty material; it may be necessary to hold down the layer, either with a large stone or more usually with a peg of wood or wire. Layering is the normal method of increase for border carnations and is used for many hard-wooded plants, especially those difficult to root from cuttings. Illustrated are (*left*) a clematis, showing the tongue well opened and the peg to hold the shoot down; and (*right*) a heather plant layered by taking out a shallow trench alongside it and bending the shoots at right angles before covering again with soil.

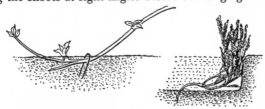

LEGUMINOUS. A member of the pea family, *Leguminosae*. The basic common character of these is the production of a legume, or pod (*left*). Most of the genera we grow in our gardens have flowers like a pea (*above, right*) with an upper petal called the standard (s), two side petals known as wings (w), and two lower ones united into the keel (k), while the stamens are either all or all but one united into a tube. Owing to their fancied resemblance to butterflies these flowers are often called papilionaceous. There are, however, two other tribes of the family, one with similar but not butterfly-like flowers, such as the Judas Tree, *Cercis siliquastrum*, and one entirely different with minute flowers in heads of various shapes as in the acacias or 'mimosa' (*below, right*). All, however, have the characteristic pods, which are sometimes woody. The pods, incidentally, are not always straight as in the pea illustrated, but may be circular or spiral.

LIGHT. *See* Frame.

LIMB. Though we sometimes speak of the limbs of a tree, meaning its branches, the term has a special botanical meaning, namely the flat, expanded part of a flower calyx or corolla which has a tubular base, as in the morning glory (ipomaea), illustrated under Funnelform.

55

LINEAR. A word meaning long and narrow, and usually applied to leaves of this shape. It is sometimes seen as a specific name, as in *Sedum lineare*, (illustrated).

LIP. A lip is, botanically, a single segment, or the result of two or more segments of a flower perianth uniting, to form a distinctive flat lobe, quite separate from the other segments. Where several upper and several lower segments have combined to make separate lips, the flower is called bilabiate. Botanists sometimes use the Latin equivalents labellum for lip and labiate for lipped, and the latter

has given its name to the family *Labiatae*, in which the flowers are often lipped, as in *Salvia patens* (*left*). The lip as a floral feature is most pronounced in the orchid family, in which the lowest petal is usually lip-shaped, sometimes exaggeratedly so as in the miltonias (*right*).

MAIDEN. A tree or bush in its first year after grafting or budding, and before any formative pruning has been carried out. This term is mainly applied to fruit trees—a maiden apple is illustrated— but also to roses and sometimes to other trees and shrubs. The lateral growths are sometimes referred to as 'feathers' and advertisements may offer 'well-feathered maidens', meaning one-year trees with plenty of side-growths. *See also* Lateral.

MONOCARPIC. This term, literally meaning once-fruiting, describes plants which die after fruiting, but take a variable time to reach flowering age. It is not normally applied to annuals, but to plants which grow from year to year in a vegetative state until they flower, fruit and die. Before doing so they often produce offsets around the flowering rosette. The so-called Century Plant, *Agave americana*, is an excellent example; it may take fifty years (or more or less) before it blooms. Most of the Bromeliads (e.g. billbergia, vriesia, aechmea) are monocarpic. Coming nearer home one may cite *Saxifraga longifolia* (illustrated) as monocarpic; this European alpine may take three to six years before flowering. Sempervivums (houseleeks) are again monocarpic. The word should not be confused with the botanical term monocarpous, meaning an ovary of a single carpel.

MONOECIOUS. *See* Dioecious.

MONSTROUS. *See* Cristate.

MORAINE. *See* Scree.

MOSAIC. *See* Virus.

MUCRONATE, MUCRONULATE. Mucronate is a botanical term, usually applied to leaves, meaning ending abruptly in a short, stiff point. Mucronulate, which is hardly different, means ending in a small, sharp point. Both words have been used as specific names, as in *Erigeron mucronatus* and *Rhododendron mucronatum* and *R. mucronulatum*.

MULCH. Any appreciable topdressing applied to the soil is called a mulch. Mulches usually consist of fairly bulky organic materials such as strawy, partly decayed manure, chopped straw, grass mowings, peat or compost. They are applied partly as food material and partly to conserve soil moisture by reducing surface evaporation. The looser the material the more it will prevent evaporation. At the same time mulches can smother weeds, and in fact avoid the need for hoeing. They also keep the soil surface cooler in summer, which encourages soil bacteria and deters certain pests.

Mulches have certain disadvantages: they absorb so much moisture that they can prevent light rain or watering from reaching the soil, so that if water must be given to the mulched plants it should be in good quantity. By the same token the soil should be thoroughly moist before a mulch is applied. In winter the temperature above the mulch will be lower than that over bare soil. Strawberries mulched with straw are therefore often covered with the material if a frosty night threatens, and uncovered in the morning, to avoid frost damage to the blossom.

The latest development in mulching is to use strips of polythene film or aluminium foil. Though these do not add food to the soil they have all the other advantages of vegetable mulches and also, by absorbing or reflecting the sunlight, improve the growing conditions around plants.

MUTATION. *See* Sport.

MYCELIUM. *See* Fairy Ring; Fungus.

NECTARY. A great number of plants have glandular tissues which secrete a sugary juice, virtually indistinguishable from honey, and sometimes known as nectar. When these are concentrated into a specific organ the latter are known as nectaries, and in some are housed in structures such as the spur of the columbine (illustrated), the pocket-like cup at the base of buttercup petals, the small pits on tulip stamens, or the round cups at the base of crown imperial petals in which large drops of fluid are held in apparent defiance of the laws of gravity. But in many other cases the nectary may be a large cushion of tissue, often towards the base

of the flower, or the sweet secretion may be spread over undefined areas of petals, sepals and other floral parts. Nectaries can also occur on leaves or stems. In most cases the nectar is undoubtedly present to attract insects to the vicinity of the stamens so that pollen will be carried from flower to flower, but nectaries outside the flowers are probably more in the nature of glands secreting unwanted substances.

NICKING AND NOTCHING. The removal of a small crescent or triangle of bark above a dormant bud will often stimulate it into growth, while the same operation below the bud, or the mere pressing of a knife into the wood there, will inhibit its growth. The former is often called notching and the latter nicking, though some authorities use the terms indiscriminately. Instead of making a cut below a bud it can be cut or rubbed out if growth is not required from it for some reason. Notching to promote growth of specific buds on fruit trees—perhaps wanted for formative purposes—is best done in early May. *See also* Bud.

NODE. *See* Joint.

NODULE. Plants cannot apparently make much use of nitrogen in the atmosphere: they normally obtain nitrogen via nitrates or similar compounds. Certain bacteria possess the power of 'fixing' gaseous nitrogen. These bacteria live in the soil, and some of them will infect the roots of any leguminous plant such as the clover illustrated. The infected cells are stimulated to grow into swellings or nodules, in which the bacteria multiply. Nitrogen diffuses through the plant, and the bacteria capture it, using some for their own purposes but releasing a good deal in such a way that the plant can employ it as food substance. In exchange, as it were, the bacteria obtain energy-providing carbohydrates from the plant.

This curious phenomenon enables leguminous plants—and one or two others—to grow happily in soils containing no available nitrogen and, what is more, a soil will usually be richer in available nitrogen after leguminous plants have been grown in it. Hence the common practice of growing lucerne or clovers in any kind of farming rotation, which are used for fodder as well as improving the soil by ploughing in the roots; and of growing and later digging in a leguminous green crop such as tares or lupins, which not only provides humus but a supply of nitrogen compounds.

NUT. A nut is technically a seed with a distinct outer shell, known as the pericarp, and a thinner skin over the seed-leaves themselves; this skin and the pericarp are separated by a cavity. Most nuts are contained either entirely or partially in an outer structure known

as the cupule, which may hold one or more nuts. The illustration shows a vertical section of an acorn, in which the cupule is the familiar acorn-cup (itself botanically the result of bracts fusing together). Other familiar nuts are hazel, beech and sweet chestnut, the latter two having cupules which entirely surround the seeds. Many seeds which are commonly called nuts, such as the horse chestnut, walnut and brazil nut, are not technically nuts at all in the botanical sense.

OBOVATE. *See* Oval.

OPPOSITE. A term usually applied to leaves which are produced in pairs on opposite sides of the stem. Opposite leaves are sometimes produced all in the same plane along a shoot, or, as in the carnation illustrated, in pairs facing opposite ways, when they can be termed decussate. Whether leaves are opposite, alternate or whorled is an important diagnostic feature in artificial keys to the identification of plants. *See also* Alternate; Whorl.

OVAL, OVATE, OBOVATE
Terms usually used in describing leaves, and all sometimes seen Latinised in specific names. Oval (*left*) means basically egg-shaped. In an ovate leaf (*centre*) the

shape is roughly oval (being pointed, blunt-ended, tapering, etc., as the case may be) but its widest point is nearer the leaf-stem than the tip of the leaf. Obovate (*right*) is the inverse of this: it means egg-shaped with the maximum width nearer the tip than the stalk. Oval and ovate may be combined with other words, as in ovate-lanceolate, long-oval, and so on.

OVARY, OVULE. The ovary is that part of the flower containing the ovules which, after fertilisation, develop into the seeds. There may be one or more ovaries, each with its own styles and stigmas. The illustration shows a vertical section of an almond flower, the single ovule in its ovary with single style clearly visible below the level of calyx, petals and the ring of stamens. *See also* Fertilisation; Pistil.

PALMATE. Shaped like an open hand—from the Latin palma, the palm of the hand. As a botanical term it is usually applied to leaves with spreading finger-like divisions or lobes, and is sometimes used as a specific name, as in *Acer palmatum* (illustrated). The word digitate has a similar meaning but usually refers to leaves in which several separate leaflets are united to a common stalk.

PAN. The more important meaning of pan, horticulturally, is in describing a hard horizontal layer in the soil, usually impermeable to air and moisture, and hence harmful to plant growth by impeding roots or drainage. Pans can be both natural and induced: a natural pan often occurs in soils in which there is a lot of iron (c). Otherwise, heavy soils are most liable to panning. A surface pan, in which the soil surface becomes smooth and hard, may occur after heavy rain (a), and can be aggravated by walking on the soil, or rolling it, before it has dried out. Farmers are familiar with what is known as a plough sole (b), due to constant ploughing to the same depth, when the soil below the furrow is compacted; and other kinds of cultivator sometimes create a similar pan if persistently used, especially on sticky soils.

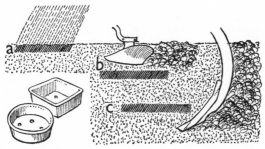

If a serious pan exists or has been created, steps must be taken to break it up. On agricultural land a sub-soiler is often used (c, *right*), a hook-shaped instrument, dragged through the soil by a tractor, which penetrates up to 18 in. deep. In the garden, deep digging or trenching must be resorted to, while hoeing and forking will destroy surface pans. Adequate humus and gritty materials help to prevent surface pans and plough soles.

The word pan is also applied to earthenware plant receptacles which are much wider than deep (*left, below, on sketch*, p. 61). They may be any width from about 3 in. (when they are sometimes known as half-pots) to 12 in., round, square or oblong. Apart from being very useful for seed sowing, they are valuable for plants with spreading or surface roots, or bulbs; in these cases a considerable depth of soil would merely stagnate and be harmful.

PANICLE. A certain type of flower-head consisting of several branches, each with a number of stalked flowers, the youngest appearing at the top of each branch as new flowers are produced.

The adjective paniculate may be Latinised as a specific name, as *Hydrangea paniculata* and *Phlox paniculata*, the species from which the herbaceous garden phlox (illustrated) is derived. In the phlox the subsidiary flower stems are opposite, but in many panicles they are alternate, as shown in the sketch at right.

PAPILIONACEOUS. *See* Leguminous.

PAPPUS. *See* Composite.

PARASITE. A parasite is an organism which lives upon another living organism. There are many parasites in the plant world. Some are complete parasites, like the dodder (cuscuta), broomrape (orobanche) and toothworth (lathraea) (all British natives)—that is, they rely entirely on the host plant for nourishment, having no leaves, nor roots capable of absorbing food from the soil. The mistletoe (viscum) (illustrated) cannot live except in association with a suitable host, into which it sends absorptive 'sinkers' (see section of parasite and tree branch at right); but it does have leaves capable of manufacturing food and is not, therefore, a complete

parasite. Other plants, such as the alpine louseworts (pedicularis) are semi-parasitic, and can exist for periods without a host. Parasitic plants have many different ways of obtaining nourishment from a host, of which the sinkers of the mistletoe are only one; some, like the Malayan rafflesia, which has the biggest flower in the world, live entirely within the tissues of the host except when flowering. *See also* Fungus; Saprophyte.

PARTERRE. Parterre is a French word which was introduced to Britain in the seventeenth century, and denotes any level garden area containing ornamental flower beds of whatever shape and size. In the sixteenth century such gardens were highly developed by the French and Italians. The parterre was usually a separate unit, most frequently rectangular, divided from the rest of the garden by stone balustrades or clipped hedges. The individual beds were often designed as knots. The word knot in the garden sense originated in 1494 and refers to a bed laid out in an intricate pattern of low-growing or clipped plants—such as box, santolina or thrift. The area around and between the clipped plants might be filled with flowering plants, but often, especially in Elizabethan days when bedding plants were unknown, left as bare soil or filled with turf, gravel, or coloured sand or soil. The knot, of course, remains a permanent decorative feature which compensates for lack of colour in off-seasons. The illustration shows a parterre with beds laid out as knots.

PARTHENOCARPIC. Fruits produced without fertilisation are termed parthenocarpic. A notable horticultural example is the greenhouse cucumber, which should in fact not be pollinated, because if seeds are produced the fruits are bitter (the opposite is

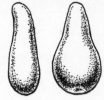

true of outdoor cucumbers). The banana is similar; indeed the cultivated banana never sets seed, and is propagated entirely by suckers. A number of plants, notably hawkweeds and their relations, are exclusively parthenocarpic, and the ovules cannot in fact be fertilised, yet the plants produce viable seed. This is really a kind of vegetative reproduction since sex does not enter into it. Parthenocarpic fruits can sometimes be produced by applying tiny quantities of plant hormones to the flowers; this has been used on tomatoes and with some success on strawberries. To be able to do this artificially is often of use when pollination conditions are poor. Something similar occurs to apples and pears which are damaged by frost in the fruitlet stage so that the ovules are killed, though not the fleshy receptacle which develops into the fruit. These fruits may be shrunken or deformed, with few or no pips. Conference pear can produce a heavy crop of seedless fruit in this way; the pipless pears are characteristically sausage-shaped (*left*, in comparison with a normal fruit).

PEDICEL, PEDUNCLE, PETIOLE. Botanical terms for

various kinds of stalk. A pedicel (a) is the stalk of a single flower, especially one in a cluster: peduncle (b) means the same but is usually applied to the main stalk of a cluster. The word pedicle used to mean the same as pedicel but is now used to denote tiny stems such as sometimes support seeds or glands. A petiole (c) is a leaf stalk. The plant illustrated is an ivy-leaved pelargonium.

PELTATE. Literally meaning shield-shaped, this term is applied to leaves with the stem (petiole) joining the underside at or near the centre. The common nasturtium, *Tropaeolum majus* (illustrated), has a peltate leaf. The word is sometimes used as a specific name, as in *Saxifraga peltata*.

PERENNIAL. A plant whose life is at least three seasons (*but see* Monocarpic).

PERFOLIATE. A word applied to leaves in which the basal lobes unite around the stem, so that the latter appears to pass right through the leaf. The word is occasionally seen as a specific name, as in *Claytonia perfoliata* (illustrated).

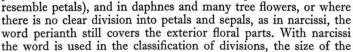

PERIANTH. The perianth of a flower comprises all the outer parts which enclose the reproductive organs, normally the calyx and corolla, which are seen to left and right in the drawing of *Cobaea scandens*. Where there is only one ring of floral parts, as in anemones and clematis (where sepals resemble petals), and in daphnes and many tree flowers, or where there is no clear division into petals and sepals, as in narcissi, the word perianth still covers the exterior floral parts. With narcissi the word is used in the classification of divisions, the size of the separate perianth segments being referred to in relation to that of the trumpet, cup or corona; both the latter and the segments comprise the perianth. *See also* Calyx; Corolla; Corona; Cup; Lip; Petal; Sepal; Trumpet.

PETAL, PETALOID. A petal is one of the divisions of the corolla of a flower, especially where this is separate from the other divisions. The corolla is usually, but not always, the showy part of a flower. Petaloid means resembling a petal, and is used for other parts of a flower which have been modified to look like petals, like the inner petals of double flowers. The word is sometimes used as a noun, the segments being referred to as petaloids, especially when they are narrower than the real petals. Petalody is the scientific name for the condition of a flower having parts modified in the form of petals. The two peonies illustrated show different degrees of petalody. *See also* Corolla; Perianth.

PETIOLE. *See* Pedicel; Tendril.

pH. *See* Calcicole.

PHYLLOCLADE. *See* Cladode.

PILOSE. *See* Hairy.

PINCHING. *See* Stopping.

PINNA, PINNATE. These words are derived from the Latin pinna, a feather or wing. In botany a pinna is one primary division —i.e., a lobe, leaflet, or subsidiary petiole (stalk) bearing separate leaflets—of a feathery, divided leaf. The term is especially used in describing ferns. The adjective pinnate describes a compound leaf or frond with a series of leaflets on each side of a common petiole. At top left is illustrated a pinnate leaf of *Sorbus aucuparia*, the mountain ash. When the leaflets themselves divide, the secondary divisions are known as pinnules (adjective pinnulate). In some cases secondary and even tertiary divisions of the petioles occur, the last

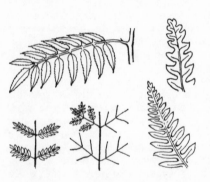

stage bearing pinnate leaflets; this division is called bipinnate (*below, left*) or tripinnate (*below, centre*). The word pinnatifid describes a lobed leaf pinnately divided at least halfway to the midrib (*top, right: Ceterach officinale*), and pinnatisect a leaf divided almost to the midrib (*below, right: Polypodium vulgare*). *See also* Frond.

PIPING. A special kind of cutting sometimes used with pinks and other dianthus, and prepared by pulling a young shoot out at a joint. A firm grip and steady pull should bring the shoot cleanly out of the lower stem, and it can then be struck exactly like an ordinary cutting, without further preparation. Pipings are usually taken in early summer from young, non-flowering shoots. *See also* Cutting.

PISTIL. The pistil comprises the entire female organ of the flower, including ovary, style and stigma. The drawing shows a section through a narcissus flower, with the pistil emphasised; the remainder comprising the stamens (the male part) and the perianth parts which enclose the sexual organs. A flower may be described as pistillate when it has pistils but no stamens, or in other words is female only. *See also* Carpel; Column; Ovary; Stigma.

PIT. In gardening, a pit was a type of frame or greenhouse which is seldom seen today, and hardly ever constructed. In pits the floor was sunk below ground level so that the frame light or greenhouse roof was at or just above soil level. The advantages of pits were that

the glass was less exposed to wind and that warmth was more easily conserved. They were often used for forcing plants, for cucumbers, and are still very valuable for propagating purposes.

PLENA, PLENIFLORA. *See* Double.

PLUNGE. Pot-grown plants are often 'plunged' outside when not wanted indoors or in the greenhouse. This means that the pots are sunk up to their rims, and it protects soil and roots from becoming too hot and from drying out. This may be done in ordinary soil, but if there are a lot of pots a special plunge bed is often made, usually of sifted boiler ashes, coarse sand or peat. Such a bed can be made above ground level with an edging of boards (*top*), and where overhead protection is also necessary the plunge bed can be made in a frame. This is usually necessary when alpines are grown in pots or pans to be taken into an alpine house when in flower. Other plants commonly plunged are hardy shrubs kept in pots for forcing, and large green-house plants which are kept out of doors during the summer.

Bulbs for indoor or greenhouse decoration in pots or bowls are normally plunged several inches deep (*below*). This ensures that they are cool and moist and that the roots develop well before much top growth, and before any forcing.

POD. *See* Capsule; Leguminous.

POLLARD. When a tree has all its boughs cut back at intervals right to the trunk it is known as a pollard, and the practice is called pollarding (from the word poll, to cut short or crop). This is sometimes done for ornament, since a few trees produce neat mop-headed growth if pollarded, but is usually carried out for

utilitarian reasons, either to keep trees within bounds or to encourage the production of a quantity of young growths, such as the 'withies' produced by pollarded willows (illustrated), much used in basket making and for the construction of hurdles. Trees which are cut back so that a number of short stumps are left—like the famous beeches in Burnham Beeches—are more correctly described as lopped. *See also* Adventitious; Stub.

POLLEN. The dust-like grains carried in the anthers of most flowering plants, which are the male sex cells. When these alight on the stigma, pollination can be said to have occurred; this is followed by the fertilisation of the ovule by the process described under Fertilisation. *See also* Anther; Column; Stigma.

POLLINATION. *See* Fertilisation; Pollen; Sterile.

POME. The technical word for the fruit of apple, pear and similar plants.

POMPON. Though used technically to denote groups of dahlias and chrysanthemums with small globular flowers, this term, derived from a French word meaning a tuft or top-knot, can be applied to other plants with such flowers.

POT. Every gardener knows what a flower pot looks like. Pots used always to be of baked clay, but nowadays plastic ones are more often seen, and there are temporary pots of 'whale-hide', compressed peat and so on through which roots can grow so that pot and all can be planted. Clay pots—which are still

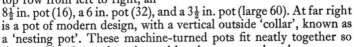

sixty 3½ in. pots are obtained from one cast, forty-eight 5 in. pots, or one 18 in. pot. From this comes the gardener's jargon of 'a small sixty', 'a forty-eight', and so on. The table below gives cast numbers with their dimensions.

Above are shown, to scale, top row from left to right, an 8½ in. pot (16), a 6 in. pot (32), and a 3½ in. pot (large 60). At far right is a pot of modern design, with a vertical outside 'collar', known as a 'nesting pot'. These machine-turned pots fit neatly together so that stacking is much easier and breakages are reduced.

The sketches below show, left, a pan, a container made in various widths, which is shallower than wide: pans can also be square or oblong. Centre, a 'long tom', a deep pot for tap-rooted plants. At right, an orchid pot, which has, besides the standard drainage holes in the base which all pots have (the larger three or more), additional holes at the side to ensure that the porous compost can never become waterlogged, and to encourage the aerial roots of many orchids to grow outside the container.

The operation of placing plants in pots is called potting and that of transferring a plant from one pot to another is repotting.

Cast size	Pot diameter	Cast size	Pot diameter
Small 72	1¾ in.	40	5½ in.
Large 72	2½ in.	32	6¼ in.
Small 60	3 in.	24	7½ in.
Large 60	3½ in.	16	8½ in.
54	4¼ in.	12	10 in.
48	5 in.		

PRICKING OUT. This rather odd expression, derived from the action of pricking small holes in the soil, and alternatively rendered as pricking off, refers to the operation of transferring seedlings from the receptacles in which they have been raised from seed to other receptacles or beds where they are given more room. This move must be done with care, because tiny seedlings are fragile, and their leaves and roots are easily damaged. Research has shown that seedlings are best moved when they have developed

their seed leaves but not their
first true leaves, since less
check to growth occurs from
a shift at the earlier stage.
Some instrument, such as a
sharp label or a label cut into
two prongs like a miniature
fork, is often useful to lever
up the seedlings; they should
be held by a seed-leaf and
placed into a hole previously
made by a dibber, after which
soil is replaced round the

roots and gently firmed. It is best to plant the pricked out seedlings
at regular intervals in rows. *See also* Dibber.

PRICKLE. *See* Spine.

PROLIFEROUS. *See* Viviparous.

PROPAGATION. Plants can be increased in a great number of
ways, that from seed being the most typical in nature (*see* Cotyledon; Germination; Pricking Out; Stratification). Garden plants
do not always breed true from seed (*see* Genus; Hybrid; Strain;
Variety), so they are increased vegetatively, that is by using parts
of the existing plant (*see* Clone). For some of these methods *see*
Air Layering; Budding; Cutting; Division; Grafting; Inarching;
Layering; Scion; Strike and Stub.

PRUNING. Pruning is an omnibus term which refers to any
cutting back of woody plants, especially fruit and ornamental trees,
bushes and shrubs. There are four main reasons for pruning: (1)
to shape the plant according to one's requirements; (2) to remove
unnecessary parts of the plant so that its energies are concentrated
where needed, or to keep it within bounds; (3) to remove dead,
damaged or diseased parts; and (4) to control the quantity and
quality of flowers and/or fruits produced.

Fruit pruning is a highly specialised subject and there are
numerous different methods, and differing shapes of tree, which
cannot be dealt with here except to say that pruning for shaping
must normally be done when the tree is young. With both fruiting
and flowering plants it is important to distinguish between those
which flower and fruit on old wood and those which do so mainly
on new wood. Black currants, raspberries and many rambler roses,
for instance, have their cropping stems cut out each year, since

the best flowers and fruits are carried on year-old stems; but most top fruits, red currants and climbing roses flower and fruit on side growths from at least a semi-permanent framework of branches.

Perhaps the commonest garden plant which is regularly pruned is the rose. It is usual to cut back hybrid teas each year, and one 'school' prunes very hard (*top, right*), though many people nowadays cut more lightly (*below, right*), which produces more shapely bushes (*left*, before pruning). Floribunda roses are always pruned lightly.

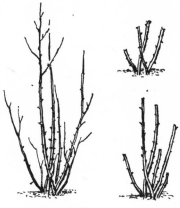

It is important to realise that any cutting back into healthy wood will promote new shoot growth from dormant buds, and in general the harder the cutting the more vigorous the resulting growth. Some ornamental shrubs can be pruned almost to ground level each spring, like the buddleia, and then produce very strong, upright new stems.

Pruning is usually carried out with secateurs, though skilled fruit growers use a special strong knife. A saw is used for large branches. *See also* Bud; Lateral; Snag.

PUBESCENT, PUBERULENT. *See* Hairy.

PUDDLING. This is an old practice in which the roots of plants being transplanted are dipped into a thick mixture of soil and water. It is supposed to help the plants to 'get away' quicker, especially in dry weather, and it is also believed to protect plants against pests such as cabbage root fly. The latter belief is almost certainly unfounded, and it is to be doubted whether puddling has much effect as protection against drought, though it can do no harm. It would seem more effective to fill the planting hole with water and let it drain before putting in the plant.

PULVERULENT. *See* Farina.

PYRAMID. The name for a form of fruit tree. The pyramid proper, which may reach 25 ft., is now seldom seen; it was often used for pears but is not very suitable for apples. The dwarf pyramid, reaching a maximum of about 7 ft., can be applied to

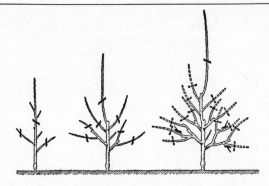

apples and is being used increasingly in intensive commercial plantations, as well as being very convenient for the garden. In the pyramid and dwarf pyramid branches radiate horizontally, starting close to the ground, from an upright central trunk, the tree eventually becoming more or less conical in outline. The drawings show the first three years of forming a dwarf pyramid apple from a feathered maiden, the heavy bars indicating cuts in winter pruning, the dotted bars those in summer pruning. In later years less wood needs to be removed.

RACEME. A botanical term for an elongated, unbranched flower-head in which each flower has a short individual stalk. The growing point continues to add to the inflorescence (up to a point) as the lower flowers open, and hence there is no terminal bud and the flowers commonly open from the base upwards, as shown in the diagram sketch, and the foxglove also illustrated. The hyacinth also has a racemose inflorescence, but here most of the flowers open at once.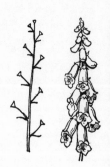

RADICAL. *See* Basal.

RAY. *See* Composite; Umbel.

RECURVED, REFLEXED. Botanical terms meaning curved or bent downwards, and applicable to leaves, petals and so on.

Recurved means gently curved, while reflexed, which is more often used, indicates a sharper downward bend. This word is indeed used by the National Chrysanthemum Society in their official classification of the different types of flower: a Reflexed Decorative is illustrated. This is the opposite of Incurved and Incurving, *which see.*

RETICULATE. A word of Latin origin which means netted—for example, with net-like, crosswise veins or markings—and is commonly applied to leaves, as in the alpine willow, *Salix reticulata*, which has veins in a net pattern. The illustration shows a flower of the orchid *Vanda caerulea* with reticulate markings of deeper blue on a pale blue ground.

REVERSION. There are two distinct gardening meanings of this word. The most general refers to a plant reverting to its original type. This sometimes happens to highly bred hybrids, which may produce flowers of different colours to those the variety is supposed to have. Some complaints of reversion, however, are not justified. One often hears of lupins 'reverting' to blue: but what has happened is that the short-lived coloured hybrid has died and seedlings from it have produced blue flowers. In cases where a grafted rose, rhododendron, lilac, etc., 'reverts' this is due to the more vigorous stock having been allowed to sucker and swamp the scion or grafted variety. A similar thing may happen with variegated plants, which are often unstable like the tradescantia illustrated (*below*). Green shoots which may be formed are much more vigorous than the variegated and if allowed to grow will swamp the latter.

In its other meaning reversion is the name for a specific virus disease of currants which reduces cropping, and in which the leaves are smaller and carry fewer lobes, with fewer veins (*top, right*) than in a normal plant (*top, left*). If a currant is suspected of infection, the leaf veins should be counted in mid-summer. If most leaves have five veins or fewer the bush is probably affected. *See also* Sucker; Virus.

RHIZOME. A rhizome is an underground stem. Rhizomes, which normally grow horizontally, are of two kinds. The thick, fleshy ones like those of bearded irises (*right*) and Solomon's Seal, and the thinner but still fleshy ones of wood anemones, are storage organs like tubers and bulbs, which enable the plant to have a resting season. These fleshy rhizomes usually produce buds and new growths at the ends; the older portions, which bear the scars left by previous years' leaves or shoots, and on which the roots deteriorate, can be discarded from time to time. The other kind of rhizome is more like an overground runner or stolon, and produces shoots at a distance from the parent, which then root themselves. Couch grass and many bent grasses grow in this way, like *Agrostis stolonifera* (*left*), a form of which is sold as a grass for planting rather than sowing. *See also* Runner; Stolon.

RIDGING. This is a method of soil cultivation in which the soil is thrown up into ridges, in order to expose as much surface as possible to the effects of frost and weather generally. Strips of ground about 30 in. wide are marked out, and a trench a spit deep and 1 ft. wide is taken out at one end, the soil being removed to the other end of the plot. The gardener works backwards from this trench, at each move back throwing three spadefuls of soil forward so as to pile the left- and right-hand spadefuls on the centre one, as seen in the diagram (*left*). The soil should not be touched with the spade again, being left as rough as possible, but if it is very friable the result will be more or less triangular ridges (*right*). At the end of each strip, the gardener turns round and works back down the next strip. *See also* Spit.

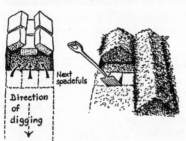

RINGING. In a tree the chemicals extracted from the soil by the roots rise in the sap via the trunk, while the food made in the leaves with the aid of these soil chemicals travels down to the roots in a layer of cells—the phloem—just beneath the bark. If this layer is cut through root growth is reduced, and this in turn eventually reduces wood growth. By doing this deliberately to a fruit tree excessive vigour and production of too much wood are curtailed, and formation of flower-buds, and hence more fruit, is encouraged.

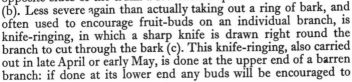

There are several ways of doing this. A ring of bark not more than ¼ in. wide can be taken out (a), right to the hard wood beneath, round the trunk about 2 ft. above the soil level. This should be done in late April or early May, which will allow the ring to heal over during the summer. A wider ring will not heal over, which would result in the tree's eventual death. A less drastic check can be given by taking out a partial ring, or two semi-circular rings on opposite sides of the trunk a few inches apart (b). Less severe again than actually taking out a ring of bark, and often used to encourage fruit-buds on an individual branch, is knife-ringing, in which a sharp knife is drawn right round the branch to cut through the bark (c). This knife-ringing, also carried out in late April or early May, is done at the upper end of a barren branch: if done at its lower end any buds will be encouraged to remain dormant.

ROGUE. Any plant with characters which are not what they are meant to be is termed a rogue. This may happen with named varieties or with seed strains which are supposed to be true: with the latter it is quite possible for a few plants to diverge from the required character from natural causes; thus a strain of blue larkspur may easily produce one or two pink ones. In other cases, as where a tulip of the wrong form or colour appears (illustrated),

or a potato of the wrong variety comes up, this is usually due to accidental mixing of the bulbs or tubers at some stage in the sorting and packing. Of course, such plants, and also perennials or shrubs normally propagated vegetatively, may occasionally differ from the original by 'sporting'. *See also* Sport.

ROOTSTOCK. A subterranean stem, often vertical. *See also* Crown; Rhizome.

ROSETTE. Originally meaning an ornament, either painted, sculptured or moulded, or made of ribbons or leather strips, which resembles a rose, the word rosette is applied botanically to any similar arrangement of petals or especially leaves in a rose-like pattern. Many alpines, such as saxifrages, have leaf rosettes, and it is also a typical leaf arrangement of succulents such as the echeverias (illustrated).

ROTATION. In the vegetable garden rotation involves changing the position of crops each year so that the same crop does not occupy the same ground in consecutive years. In this way any build-up of pests and diseases peculiar to one plant is reduced, and the best use is made of plant foods in the soil—some crops needing fresh manure or fertilisers, others preferring ground which has been manured for an earlier crop. Farmers have observed rotation for centuries with individual crops; the limited space of the average garden or allotment makes it simpler to avoid a rigid rotation and to group plants of a similar type together.

The diagram illustrates a simple three-year rotation. The groups of crops, which are alternated as shown in years 1, 2, and 3, are as follows:

(A) All brassicas except those in B, which may be preceded by, or intercropped with, lettuces, radishes and other salad crops. This plot should be dressed with animal manure or compost, and limed at a separate time, while the growing crops may be fed with nitrate of soda or sulphate of ammonia.

(B) Potatoes to be followed by broccoli, spring cabbage, coleworts, leeks and late-sown turnips. This plot is dressed with manure or compost but not lime, and if potatoes are grown a balanced fertiliser should be applied just before planting.

(C) Rootcrops: Carrots, parsnips, turnips and beetroot. Peas and beans intercropping with summer spinach and lettuce. Of these only the peas and beans need manure, but wood ashes may be worked in and a complete fertiliser applied just before sowing.

1	2	3
A	C	B
B	A	C
C	B	A
D	D	D

(D) Onions, which often grow best if left permanently in the same plot. If they are to be rotated, they should go into group C. This plot needs manure or compost and wood ashes, and the onions may be fed with nitrate of soda after thinning.

RUGOSE. A botanical term meaning wrinkled, and usually applied to leaves with a wrinkled surface. It is sometimes Latinised as a specific name, as in *Rosa rugosa* (illustrated).

RUNNER. Among the specialised shoots plants produce for vegetative reproduction is the runner, a slender stem growing on the surface of the ground and making roots from the buds which occur at intervals along it. The strawberry is a well-known example which the gardener likes, and the creeping buttercup a notorious example of a weed, for the rooted plantlets soon become large enough to throw out more runners around themselves. Another garden plant with runners is the violet (illustrated). When garden plants such as the strawberry (*see* Clone for illustration) and

the violet produce runners, they should be cut off unless wanted for increase, as otherwise they may weaken the parent and overcrowd the bed. Runners selected for propagation should be limited in number and only the first plantlet formed allowed to develop. *See also* Adventitious; Node; Rhizome; Stolon.

SAGITTATE. Literally meaning arrow-shaped, this word is used to describe leaves in the shape of an arrow-head, that is triangular, pointed, and with two backward-pointing lobes. The water plant sagittaria has been named for its normally arrow-shaped leaves: two forms of the very variable *S. sagittifolia* are illustrated.

SAPROPHYTE. A saprophyte is a plant which lives on decaying matter. (The word is derived from Greek words meaning 'putrid' and 'plant'.) As a result—and like many parasitic plants which live on living organisms—these saprophytes contain no chlorophyll and are unable to manufacture food with the aid of sunlight. The biggest groups of saprophytes are found among the fungi, both

large and microscopic, and the bacteria. The common mushroom (*top*, *left*) is one, and so are some of the smaller bracket fungi (*centre*: polyporus species) which are seen on broken branches and tree stumps, though most bracket fungi are harmful parasites. Compost heaps often contain white threadlike growths, which are the vegetative part of saprophytic fungi. These are beneficial and cannot harm living plants. Several higher plants are also indirectly saprophytic, such as the brown, leafless Bird's Nest Orchid (neottia) (*right*) and the Yellow Bird's Nest (monotropa, of the heath family), which are quite common in Britain. These plants cannot make use of decaying matter directly, but their mass of roots (which are more or less like a bird's nest—hence the names) are entered by a saprophytic fungus. The fungus provides starch for the plant, and there may be some reciprocal benefit; such an association is termed symbiosis. *See also* Fungus; Parasite; Symbiosis.

SCALDING. *See* Shanking.

SCAPE. A scape is a flower stem which grows directly from ground level and bears no leaves. In *Amaryllis belladonna* (illustrated) there are, indeed, normally no leaves to be seen at flowering time. Hippeastrums and clivias also carry their flowers on scapes, in these cases arising from the bulb or crown of the plant.

SCION, STOCK. Scion is the term for any shoot or bud separated from one individual plant and joined to another in order to form a composite plant. The plant to which the shoot or bud is joined, by grafting or budding, is known as the stock, and provides the root system, whereas the scion provides all the aerial shoots or branches, and any growth emanating from the stock must be removed; apart from being unwanted it may be more vigorous than the scion growth and swamp it. In the illustration of what is known as the saddle graft, commonly used for rhododendrons, the scion is, of course, uppermost. The plants which are most commonly budded or grafted are roses and fruit trees. The method is used to ensure rapid growth of varieties of choice hybrid plants which cannot be increased true from seed and which are either slow or impossible to grow from cuttings, or have undesirable growth habits when on their own roots. This is particularly so with fruit trees, which fruit quickly after being grafted, and in which a range of carefully selected stocks controls the ultimate size and vigour of the tree in relation to the soil. *See also* Budding; Grafting; Sucker.

SCORPIOID. *See* Cyme.

SCREE, MORAINE. A scree in nature is the mass of rock debris which collects at the foot of a mountain or cliff, while a moraine is the similar rocky accumulation at the snout or at the sides of glaciers, which has been produced by the grinding action of the glacier on rock. In nature both have a characteristic flora of plants which enjoy very sharp drainage and a minimum of humus. Despite their extreme porosity moraines and screes are usually damp when melting snow above provides ample moisture.

There is no sharp difference between the two when imitated in a garden, but the word moraine is usually used for beds mainly of small stones which can be provided with water from below, and scree reserved for similar arrangements not watered from below. The illustration shows the arrangement of a moraine bed, which is preferably sloping, with a good layer of coarse drainage material about a foot deep, covered with inverted turves to prevent the upper layer from working down. This layer, about 2 ft. deep, will vary in content according to the plants to be grown, but a general-purpose mixture contains 10 parts (by bulk) of coarse stone chippings (limestone or granite according to the needs of the plants), 1 part good loam, 1 part sphagnum moss and 1 part coarse sand, but much more loam can be included. Rocks may be bedded in the surface. When watering from below is intended, a pipe with very small holes, quite widely spaced, should be buried about a foot down, and connected with a water supply. It is mainly used in hot weather. The scree or moraine is ideal for most alpine plants and is often the only way of growing difficult ones.

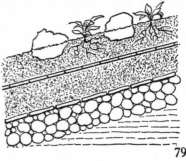

SEED LEAF. *See* Cotyledon.

SELECTION. *See* Strain.

SELECTIVE. Applied to certain weedkillers, mainly but not entirely those known as hormone weedkillers, which can be used to kill broadleaved weeds in lawns, among crops related to the grasses, and in certain other circumstances. The materials usually used for lawns are 2, 4-D and MCPA, while more powerful materials known as brushwood killers, capable of destroying brambles and scrub among trees, are based on 2, 4, 5-T. *See also* Hormone.

SEMI-DOUBLE. *See* Double.

SEPAL. Where the outer parts of a flower—which together form the calyx—are more or less separate, they are known as sepals. Though in some cases, like waterlilies and many cacti, the sepals may resemble the petals, or, as in the clematis and anemones, may actually replace them and be brightly coloured, they are usually green or brownish, even scale-like, and enclose the flower bud protectively before it opens. They are normally smaller than the

expanded petals. The illustration shows a flower (*left*) of the cloudberry (*Rubus chamaemorus*), showing the slightly hairy sepals which persist when the fruit ripens (*right*). *See also* Calyx; Perianth.

SERRATE, SERRULATE. *See* Toothed.

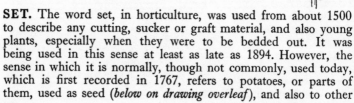

SESSILE. This botanical term simply means stalkless, and refers to leaves, or flowers such as those of *Daphne mezereum* (illustrated) which have no stalks and spring directly from the shoots.

SET. The word set, in horticulture, was used from about 1500 to describe any cutting, sucker or graft material, and also young plants, especially when they were to be bedded out. It was being used in this sense at least as late as 1894. However, the sense in which it is normally, though not commonly, used today, which is first recorded in 1767, refers to potatoes, or parts of them, used as seed (*below on drawing overleaf*), and also to other

80

tuberous plants, onions and occasionally shallots for planting.

The word is also used to describe blossom which has been fertilised and is starting to ripen fruit or seed, when the flowers are said to have set (*above*). The expression 'a good set of fruit' derives from this.

SETOSE. *See* Hairy.

SHANKING. A physiological trouble of ripening grapes, in which the small individual stalks of each berry wither, so that the grapes themselves, deprived of nourishment, dry up in their turn.

 It is usually due to the soil in which the vine is growing becoming waterlogged or impoverished, and it is often necessary to remake the border entirely, paying special attention to drainage. Shanking should not be confused with scalding, in which the berries, but not the stalks, go brown and collapse due to sun scorch.

SHRUB. A plant whose stems are mainly woody, or fruticose, as botanists call it. A shrub is usually taken to be a plant with many stems rather than the single trunk of a tree, but the borderline between large shrubs and small trees is not always easy to define. *See also* Sub-shrubby.

SIDE-SHOOT. *See* Lateral.

SINGLE. *See* Double.

SINGLING. *See* Thinning.

SNAG. In any pruning or cutting back of branches on shrubs or trees it is important to cut or saw cleanly back to the trunk or larger branch, to avoid leaving any rough, broken wood or short stumps. A rough wound forms a ready point for infection by diseases such as silver leaf. Stumps of branches may decay likewise or, especially on fruit and ornamental trees, will often sprout long, thin shoots the following year (*left*), which are usually useless and misplaced, and simply absorb the plant's energies. Snags left in rose pruning (*right*) above the selected bud which will grow out the following summer (dotted lines), inevitably dry up and may become a point of infection. The black bar shows the correct point to prune. *See also* Pruning; Water Shoots.

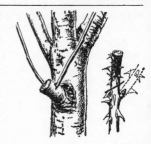

SOIL BLOCK. A fairly recent invention in which soil is compressed into blocks, round, square or hexagonal, produced in some kind of mechanical device, of which many types exist. Seeds are planted in the centre of these blocks, which are roughly equivalent to a $3\frac{1}{2}$ in. pot, and the seedlings grow in them and are planted out complete with the block. Normal potting compost should be used, but it must be a little moister than for normal potting. A well-made block should cohere until planting-out time. Soil blocks are very convenient, save the expense of pots and reduce transplanting checks. The sketches show, left to right, making a soil block; sowing a seed in a pocket of compost at the top; and a plant grown in a soil block. Prefabricated peat blocks can be purchased; with these the depression at the top is filled with compost.

SPADIX, SPATHE. The spadix is a special kind of flower spike found in aroids and palms. The insignificant flowers are usually embedded into its surface, as in anthuriums, or less often project from it, as in our native Lords and Ladies, *Arum maculatum* (illustrated; flower cut open at base). In the arums the spadix (S) projects beyond the flowers in the form of a club; in *A. maculatum* it has bristles above the flowers which trap insects to ensure pollination. Here again both male and female flowers are carried

together; it is more common for the spadix to be unisexual. In palms the spadix is often branched.

The spathe is a bract which encloses one or several flowers. It usually occurs in plants with a spadix, but not always; the sheath which surrounds a daffodil bud is technically a spathe. In arums the spathe (SP) is leafy and more or less fleshy, sometimes brightly coloured as in anthuriums, while in palms it is fleshy or even woody, and sometimes with several divisions. *See also* Aroid; Stipule.

SPATULATE. This word—also spelt spathulate—means spatula-shaped, that is, having one rounded, broadened end and narrowing abruptly at the opposite end. In botany it is applied to leaves or petals of this form and is sometimes used as a specific name, as in *Sedum spathulatum* and S. *spathulifolium*. The illustration shows the succulent *Aeonium arboreum*, which has markedly spatulate leaves.

SPAWN. *See* Fungus.

SPECIES. *See* Genus.

SPIKE. Though this word is loosely used by gardeners to refer to any elongated flower-head, such as that of a delphinium, it technically means an elongated flower cluster in which the individual flowers are more or less sessile, that is stalkless (*left*). Delphinium florets have short stalks and the delphinium flower-head is therefore technically a raceme. The mullein (verbascum) illustrated (*right*) has sessile flowers in a spike.

The word spikelet is a botanical term for the flowers of grasses; here the spikelets, which consist of several distinctive parts, are themselves arranged in spikes, racemes or panicles (*which see*).

83

SPINE. A great many plants are equipped with hard, sharp organs which are variously termed spines, thorns or prickles. Thorns are sharp woody structures which are basically modified branches, springing from the woody structure of the plant, usually more or less regularly arranged, and which cannot be removed without causing stem damage. Prickles are outgrowths from the outer layer, usually irregularly spaced, which can be removed without damage. The word spine usually refers to slender thorn-like growths. However, these terms have been hopelessly muddled up; the growths on cacti (*centre: Ferocactus rectispinus*) are always referred to as spines, though they are technically thorns, while the so-called thorns of a rose (*below, right: Rosa pteracantha*) are technically prickles.

Besides occurring on the stems of plants, thorns, prickles or spines may be found on leaves, as in thistles and hollies (*top, right*). Sometimes the leaves are transformed into spines, as in gorse

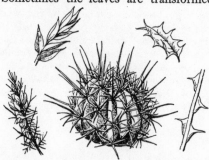

(*below, left*), or in some cases the spiny structures may replace the leaves, as in butcher's broom (*top, left*). A spiny structure is often associated with arid conditions, and is usually effective protection against animals, though this is probably a secondary effect.

SPIT. The present meaning of spit in the garden sense is a spade's depth of soil. From this we obtain expressions like single-spit digging, when the soil is dug to one's spade's (or fork's) depth only. The sketch shows a trench being dug to two spits' depth. The word originally also meant the actual thrust of the spade when digging, and the amount of soil that could be taken up by a spade; but these meanings are obsolete, as is the verb to spit meaning to dig or plant with a spade. *See also* Ridging; Trenching.

Cuckoo-spit is the name given to the frothy mass produced for self-protection by the nymphs of the frog-hopper, a sap-sucking insect that attacks many kinds of plant.

SPORE. Spores are the micro-scopic reproductive bodies of flowerless plants, which include ferns, mosses, horsetails, sela-ginellas and fungi. They are different in structure and origin in these families. The spores, though give rise to young plants as seeds do, are often asexually produced—that is, no

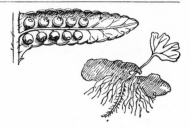

male and female cells are involved as in flowering plants—but there is then a sexual phase at another time in the plant's development.

Apart from dealing with fungus diseases which arise from spores, the gardener is only practically involved with spores if he grows ferns. Each fern produces sporangia, usually on the underside of its fronds. These are brown areas of spore-producing bodies, which are distinctively shaped in each species, and which the uninitiated sometimes believe to be a disease. At left is a single pinna (leaflet) of *Cyathea elegans*, showing the sporangia. If the frond is placed over a sheet of paper as it becomes mature, the powder-like spores are deposited on it. If these spores are sprinkled on a sterile, peaty soil mixture, in a vessel which can be covered with a sheet of glass, green flat growths will appear after a time (sometimes several months). These growths are known as prothalli. Beneath each prothallus sexual organs are formed, and the resultant male gametes fertilise the female ones. After this union the first minute frond is produced (*right*, seen from below). At this stage the tiny plants are very carefully pricked out an inch apart into a fine compost. Larger fronds will soon appear and the plants (sometimes called sporelings) are potted on in the normal way. *See also* Fern; Frond; Fungus.

SPORT. Sport is the gardener's word for what science calls a mutation, and may be defined as a spontaneous variation from an original type. Mutations occur in all kinds of living organisms. In plants these variations must not be confused with those that arise from seed of hybrid origin: sports are accidental changes in the genetical make-up of the plant, not to be produced by breeding, which can then be vegetatively increased or, if the plant is a species, will breed true. Any species or vegetatively increased variety maintains its characters by the replication of each of the numerous genes carried on its chromosomes: every now and then the mechan-ism may 'slip' and a gene be altered to a slightly different one, producing correspondingly different characters. Sports tend to occur most frequently in highly bred plants, where the genetical mechanism is apparently unstable, as with the chrysanthemum, in which numerous colour forms of individual varieties arise, and sometimes changes of form, such as reflexed to incurved. The Spencer sweet pea is a form which arose as a mutation. The illustration shows a pelargonium variety called Skelly's Pride, with fringed petals, which arose from a plain-petalled variety called Flame  (single bloom shown) to which it sometimes reverts.

In some plants, including chrysanthemums, camellias and fruits, only a part of the plant may change: this is called a bud-sport and must be carefully increased, if wanted, from the part affected only. One odd feature is that sometimes sporting of, say, a chrysanthemum variety from red to pink may occur more or less simultaneously wherever it is grown. Something similar may have happened to the musk, which lost its scent all over the world about 1914. Sporting can be induced by chemicals such as colchicine or by bombardment with X-rays or atomic particles, and may normally occur from the impact of cosmic particles.

Gardeners naturally preserve decorative or useful sports. Mutations may of course be either beneficial or harmful; in nature harmful ones will shortly perish, but beneficial ones or improvements will survive. Gene mutation is, in fact, the basic process of evolution—a series of infinitesimal jumps towards something better or more adapted to its surroundings. *See also* Chimaera; Chromosome; Rogue; Variegated; Weeping; Witch's Broom.

SPUD. Apart from its slang meaning of potato, which is first recorded in 1860, spud has since 1667 meant a digging or weeding tool with a narrow, often chisel-shaped blade. The verb to spud means to weed or dig with such a tool. Several types of spud are available today, including one with a bent blade (*left*), used either way up, and the straight 'thistle spud' (*right*). Spuds sometimes  have a hook-shaped projection on one side to help in picking up the severed weed. The spud can be mounted on a short or a long handle, and is valuable for working among plants without disturbing the soil too much.

SPUR. Horticulturally the word spur is used to describe clusters of fruit buds which develop on the older branches of fruit trees. In time these spurs branch and increase excessively, leading to small overcrowded fruits, and such ancient spurs should be reduced both in size and number by pruning in winter. Spurs are encour-

aged to form on trained trees such as cordons (illustrated), as they allow the tree to carry a good quantity of fruit in a limited space. To form a spur on a maiden tree, the laterals are cut back to four buds (*left, above*). The following year the lateral has produced some fruit buds and a new shoot: the latter is reduced to one bud (*left, below*), and this is repeated annually.

To the botanist a spur is a tubular organ which usually contains nectar, to attract pollinating insects. Such spurs are found in many orchids, columbines, toadflaxes, etc. *See* Nectary.

STAMEN. The stamen is the male organ of the flower, and is usually composed of a thin stalk, or filament, and a head, known as the anther, which actually carries and releases the pollen. Sometimes stamens have little or no stalk and the anthers are attached directly to the petals. The number of stamens varies greatly according to the family. They may become changed into petals or petaloids and this process results in double or semi-double flowers: these are most commonly found, of course, where there are numerous stamens. Families which have many stamens, and are liable to doubling, are considered by some botanists to be less highly evolved than those with fewer stamens. Stamens

are often a decorative part of the flower as in *Hypericum patulum* (*left*); while in the bottlebrushes or callistemons (*right*), acacias and other flowers the stamens may be the most prominent part of the flower.

If cross-fertilisation is being aimed at, pollen is obtained from the stamens of the chosen male parent, while the chosen female flower, or seed parent, must be emasculated by removal of the stamens at an early stage, even before bud opening, to prevent self-fertilisation.

87

A flower which has only stamens and no pistils may be called staminate, in other words is male only. *See also* Anther; Double; Emasculation; Petal.

STANDARD. To the gardener the term standard refers to any tree or shrub grown with a bare stem. In fact most large trees grow naturally in this way, but the gardener trains trees as standards from an early age, either for decorative reasons or, as with fruit trees, for utility. Roses are often grown as standards, but it is not always realised how many shrubs are effective treated like this,

particularly those of a weeping habit like the young *Cotoneaster hybrida pendula* illustrated. Such shrubs, and roses, are usually grafted when grown as standards, but plants like fuchsias and heliotropes are normally on their own stems. Standard roses are usually on 5 ft. stems and standard fruit or ornamental trees on 6 ft. stems: half-standards have shorter stems, 3 ft. to 4 ft. tall.

Botanically a standard is a part of the flower, in the iris, where it refers to the three upright petals (in contrast to the pendulous or horizontal falls), and in the sweet pea and other leguminous plants, in which the upright back petal is the standard. *See also* Beard; Grafting; Leguminous.

STERILE. Any flower incapable of producing seeds is known as sterile. Such sterile-flowered plants sometimes arise as hybrids, as in the hortensia type of hydrangea (*left on drawing opposite*), which were deliberately bred, or as sports (mutations) as in the Snowball Tree, *Viburnum opulus sterile*. The showy flowers of the hydrangea are quite sterile; an intermediate stage is seen in the type known as the lacecap (*right*) in which a ring of similar sterile flowers surrounds a centre composed of small fertile ones. In some very double flowers—double stocks, for instance—all the sexual organs are converted into petals and the flowers are sterile for this reason. Sterility is sometimes a valuable feature: thus bananas are quite seedless, and more pleasant to eat because of this; seedless raisins are another example.

On other occasions sterility can be a nuisance. Some fruit trees, such as sweet cherries, are self-sterile—that is, they cannot produce fruits as a result of self-pollination: and to crop they must receive pollen from certain other varieties. The same applies, though to a less acute degree, to apples and

pears, and those planning to grow fruit trees must ensure that varieties are chosen and interplanted which will satisfactorily pollinate each other.

STERILISATION. Completely sterile soil, deprived of all its microscopic organisms, is of little use; but partially sterilised soil, in which most fungi and all insects and weed seeds have been destroyed, but not most bacteria, is highly desirable for pot plants, especially at the germination and seedling stages when fungus diseases such as damping off so readily attack the plants. That is one reason why properly made John Innes composts are so valuable: the loam has been sterilised. It is not necessary to sterilise peat or sand, which are inert.

Sterilisation can be carried out in several ways. The most efficient is by heat, and commercial growers use high-pressure steam. A small quantity of soil can be sterilised by hanging a bag of soil in a large saucepan or other receptacle so that it is just above water level. The illustration shows a commercial product using this principle: the bag of soil (*left*) sits on a raised grid which keeps it out of the water. Boiling is carried out with a lid in place (*right*) for about 20 minutes during which time a temperature around 200°F. should be achieved. Higher temperatures,

or heat applied for too long, will destroy beneficial micro-organisms and possibly the soil structure, making the soil unable to support plant life.

Another method employs electricity passed through damp soil between metal electrodes. The resistance of the soil causes it to heat up until it is quite dry and sterilised.

89

Chemicals can also be used, notably cresylic acid and formaldehyde, the former being specially effective against insects and the latter against fungi. These chemicals are applied to the spread-out soil in solution through a rosed can, and the fumes are trapped in the soil by covering with sacks or tarpaulin. These chemicals must be used in accordance with maker's instructions, and soil cannot be used for some weeks afterwards.

STIGMA, STYLE. The stigma is that part of the pistil, or female organ of the flower, which becomes receptive to pollen, usually becoming sticky when ready. Its receptive surface is usually covered with microscopic hairs, usually glandular. The style is the channel between the stigma and the ovary, down which

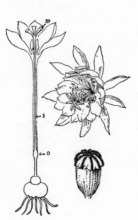

the pollen grains must grow in order to achieve fertilisation with the ovules in the ovary. Occasionally, as in the crocus (*left:* adapted from E. A. Bowles) the style (s) between the stigma (st) and ovary (o) is extremely long, but usually it is much shorter. Sometimes the style is an ornamental feature of the flower, as in the epiphyllums (*top, right*), where it has numerous branches and is shaped like a starfish supported on a medium-length style. In many plants, like the lily, there is only a single stigma. Sometimes the stigmatic surfaces are quite different in appearance and may not be carried on a style at all, as in the poppy (*below, right*) where they are arranged above the ovary in radiating lines on a circular disc. *See also* Carpel; Fertilisation; Pistil.

STIPULE. Stipules are leaf-like or scale-like organs found, in some plants only, at the base of a leaf-stalk or at a stem node. They are usually small or quite insignificant, but sometimes large enough to give some protection to the leaf bud they surround, occasionally united round the leaf-stalk or merging with it. In some cases, as in *Lathyrus aphaca*, the two leaves are reduced to tendrils and the stipules are large and act as leaves; in some desert acacias the stipules are converted into thick spiny structures. Many stipular structures are perhaps more accurately named as spathes, enclosing and protecting in a membranous envelope the young

90

leaves of trees such as oaks or beeches before they unfold. In the garden the best-known plant with stipules is the rose, where they often surround the base of the leaf-stalk, and a pair of well-defined stipules is often seen on the flower stalk (arrowed on drawing). In botany, stipules are often important identification characters.

STOCK. *See* Scion.

STOLON. Strictly, a shoot that produces a new plant at its tip, sometimes by bending down as in the blackberry, but most often stolons are horizontal stems either above or below ground. These differ from runners, which root at their nodes, but the terms are often used indiscriminately. *See also* Adventitious; Rhizome; Runner.

STOMATA. The stomata (singular stoma) are the 'breathing pores' of plants. They are microscopic openings, usually leading into a larger cavity in the underlying tissue, and carry out gaseous interchange between the plant and the atmosphere. Each stoma is surrounded by two 'guard-cells', as shown in the plan view (*left*) and section (*right*) through a leaf of *Peperomia arifolia* (magnified 350 times: after Kerner). When these guard-cells absorb water in moist conditions they become turgid, and owing to their shape and the construction of the cell walls this causes them to bulge outwards, thus increasing the size of the opening, or pore. In dry conditions this process is reversed, and the pore becomes smaller and finally closed. In this way excessive transpiration in dry conditions is prevented. The stomata are also sensitive to light, through a chemical process, tending to close in darkness.

Stomata are normally on the undersides of leaves, but on vertical leaves (such as those of irises) they may be on both sides,

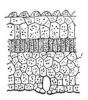

and on floating leaves (e.g. waterlilies) on the upper side only. In leafless plants such as some brooms the stomata are carried on the stems, often in grooves. In xerophytes (plants adapted to arid conditions) the stomata are relatively few in number, and may

91

be protected against excessive heat or drying winds by being sunk in small pits, or surrounded by hairs or other microscopic outgrowths.

STONE. Apart from its literal meaning of stone used for walls, rock gardens and so forth, stone is a technical term for those fruits with a succulent outer part and a hard, woody inner one, as in the peach (illustrated), plum, cherry and apricot. Botanically such fruits are included in the drupes, but the gardener calls them stone fruits. If the stones do not form properly, the fruits may be imperfect; split stone is a condition in which the kernel splits, which may be due to faulty pollination or early insect

attack; gumming of the stone is sometimes due to fluctuations in the soil moisture, or to lack of sufficient food. Lack of water, low temperatures and poor ventilation can all cause trouble during the so-called stoning period of grapes, when these seeds start to harden, though the grape seeds are not technically stones. *See also* Drupe.

STOOL. In its horticultural sense stool seems to have become confused with stolon, since it means a group of shoots emerging from the base of a single plant. In modern times its meaning is mainly restricted to plants used chiefly for propagation. The roots of chrysanthemums, after they have flowered, are known as stools,

and the following spring they will produce a number of shoots from which cuttings can be taken (illustrated).

Apple stocks are usually planted in stool beds, in well separated rows in which the young shoots can be pegged down and covered with soil so that they layer and produce roots.

In forestry a stool is the stump or stock of a tree, especially if this has been cut for the production of coppice wood or young timber.

STOPPING. To stop a plant is to remove its growing tip in order to make it produce side growths. It is particularly important with florist flowers such as chrysanthemums, dahlias and perpetual carnations, where stopping controls the number of flowers and approximate time at which they appear, as is described under Break (side growths are often described as 'breaks' by gardeners). In chrysanthemums the actual type of flower—its petalage and character—can be altered according to the type of bud induced by the stopping process: the more stopping of lateral growths made, in general, the fewer petals the flowers have.

Stopping is also important in the culture of plants such as marrows, cucumbers and vines which produce laterals freely; here stopping is desirable to encourage fruits rather than leaves, and to control the amount of growth made. In vines, for instance, the main laterals (which have been encouraged to form by spur pruning in winter) are stopped when the bunch has formed, so as to leave two leaves beyond the bunch (a). Any sub-laterals which form later as a result of this stopping are themselves stopped at one leaf (b).

The actual stopping is often carried out by pinching the stem between finger and thumb, and the word pinching is sometimes used in the same sense as stopping; but the operation can also be done with a knife, while with carnations the shoot is broken off at a joint. *See also* Crown; Topping.

STOVE. Nowadays a stove house means any greenhouse kept at a high temperature—a winter minimum of 70° or more—and used for tropical plants. High air humidity is also necessary, and such houses must be frequently damped down. A feature of the

older stove houses was a plunging bed of coconut fibre, with hot water pipes below it; in the days before hot-water heating came into general use this plunge was filled with tan-bark (waste material from tanneries) or other vegetable matter which would ferment and heat up like a huge hot-bed. Since it was desirable to conserve as much heat as possible, stove houses were often built against a wall, as shown in the sketch, which is adapted from J. C. Loudon's *Encyclopaedia of Gardening* of 1822; the plunge bed full of fermenting material is seen in the centre, with stagings at the sides.

STRAIN. Any plant increased from seed—even a wild species—will vary a certain amount. It was by using seeds of wild poppies and foxgloves that the Rev. Wilks raised his famous Shirley strains. When it comes to highly bred garden plants, variation—even in well stabilised or so-called pure-breeding varieties—is likely to be considerable unless the greatest care is taken in selecting the seed parents; without this the original variety may deteriorate. It is for this reason that vegetable seeds are constantly announced as 'Re-selected'; and for the same reason that varieties of the same name, but from different sources, may show small differences. Such selections are commonly known as strains. This is a horticultural term rather than a botanical one. The botanist's word for a strain showing sufficient differences from other strains would be a form. Growers of exhibition vegetables often select and save their own seed: many of the prize-winning onions are from home-selected strains, and the sketch shows a good strain of Ailsa Craig (*left*) with a poor one having a misshapen bulb and thick neck.

Even vegetatively produced material, such as chrysanthemums increased from cuttings, often show variations, due to mutations or to chronic diseases, and one could refer to a good type of a chrysanthemum as 'so-and-so's strain'.

The moral of all this is, of course, that to maintain a good strain, even from one year to the next, it is essential to save seeds or to obtain cuttings only from plants which show every desired characteristic of the strain. A good nurseryman or seedsman does this automatically for the customer.

STRATIFICATION. This is a process applied to certain seeds to improve and speed up germination, especially those with hard or thick, fleshy coats. Seeds of trees and shrubs frequently need stratifying. Seeds to be stratified are placed on a layer of sand in boxes, pans or pots, and covered with more sand. A mixture of sand and peat is sometimes used. Two or three layers of seed can be accommodated in a pot. The containers are then put outside in a place exposed to the elements, and left there during the winter. It is sometimes necessary, with very hard seeds (e.g., tree peonies) to leave them for eighteen months, over two winters. During the following spring the seeds are removed from the sand by sieving and are sown in the normal way. If they have fleshy coats, like rose hips, the seeds are rubbed through a sieve, or picked over with the fingers, to remove the coats. Some gardeners turn over and examine the mixture of seeds and sand once a month in the spring until there are signs of germination. The sprouting seeds are then sown in ordinary containers at the appropriate depth.

Stratification is most necessary where a fairly large number of seeds is being dealt with. If only a few seeds are involved they can be sown in the ordinary way, perhaps a little deeper than usual, fleshy ones having their coats removed manually, and left exposed to the elements over the winter months as before.

STRIG. Strig is a word of obscure origin, dating back to the sixteenth century, and meaning a stalk, whether of leaf, fruit or flower. Its only common horticultural use today is in referring to a single cluster of currants, the whole of which is spoken of as a strig.

STRIKE. In the seventeenth century a plant putting out roots was said to be striking. From this was derived the modern horticultural meaning of the word, which is to cause a cutting to root, or to increase a plant by means of cuttings. To strike a cutting, therefore, means preparing and treating a piece of plant in such a way as to encourage it to root: the drawing shows pelargonium

cuttings being suitably prepared, by trimming below a node and removing the lower leaves, prior to inserting in a suitable rooting medium in suitable atmospheric conditions. A struck cutting is one that has formed roots. The word 'take' is sometimes used in the same sense as strike. *See also* Cutting.

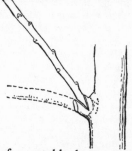

STUB. Stub has various horticultural meanings. One refers to the stump of a tree left in the ground after felling, and also sometimes to the base of the trunk of an entire tree. From this are derived the verb to stub, and an adjective: thus one speaks of stubbing out a tree, which means to dig it out roots and all, and a stubbing mattock is a tool for this job.

The word is more often used in the sense of short pieces of cut or broken branches projecting from a main stem; a pollarded tree is sometimes spoken of as stubbed, or as a stub. The fruit grower uses the term more precisely when making stub grafts (illustrated), in which scions are inserted at the base of small side branches, the latter being later removed except for the basal portion containing the graft, which is one of those used in frameworking (i.e. grafting all over an existing tree). *See also* Grafting; Pollard.

STYLE. *See* Stigma.

SUB-SOIL. *See* Trenching.

SUB-SHRUBBY. The normal meaning of sub-shrubby is in referring to a perennial plant which is woody at the base but produces, on the woody framework, soft, herbaceous growth which is liable to die in winter like the entire growth of ordinary herbaceous perennials. The common sage (illustrated in diagrammatic form: woody parts with heavy lines) is a well-known example of a sub-shrub. Many plants are of this type, notably those from hot, dry, Mediterranean-type climates; but how they behave in winter often depends on the climate in which they are grown. Thus the hardy fuchsias (*F. magellanica* type) retain most of their soft growth all

the year round in south-western England and Eire; but in districts with cold winters they are apt to be cut back, often to ground level. The Latin equivalent sub-shrubby is suffruticose, which is occasionally seen as a specific name, e.g. *Paeonia suffruticosa*. The technical name of a sub-shrub is a suffrutex.

The word is also sometimes used in the literal and basically erroneous sense of a small, low shrub. Thus there is a dwarf variety of box called *Buxus sempervirens suffruticosa*.

SUCCULENT. The word succulent derives from the Latin *succus*, meaning juice or sap: and a succulent plant is a thick, fleshy one which is usually very juicy or sappy. Though this might be taken to include bulbous and other fleshy-rooted plants, in practice it is restricted to those which have developed swollen leaves or stems as an adaptation to arid conditions, and in general to tender plants, though numerous hardy plants are also succulent, such as sedums and sempervivums.

Many families of plants have developed succulence. The cactus family is one which is almost entirely succulent; so is the mesembryanthemum family (*Aizoaceae* or *Ficoidaceae*) from South Africa. Some five other families have numerous succulent members, and about 35 others have at least one or two succulent species.

In the cactus family and the euphorbia and stapelia tribes, the tendency has been to lose leaves and develop spherical or columnar 'plant-bodies'. The sketches show other tendencies: fleshy leaves (a, *Crassula arborescens*); thick stems and small or no leaves (b, *Kleinia anteuphorbium*); the rosette (c, an echeveria); and swollen stem-base (g, adenia—a passion flower relation). In the mesembryanthemum family we can trace evolution from shrubs to plants with very thick leaves (d, a pleiospilos), to 'plant-bodies' in which the leaf pair is only just defined (e, a cheiridopsis), and those in which the leaves have merged (f, a conophytum). *See also* Cactus.

SUCKER. Any secondary growth which arises from the roots of a plant, and develops leaves of its own, is technically a sucker; this is one of the natural ways in which plants increase. Suckers spring from adventitious buds on roots of shrubs such as lilac (in diagram, *left*, *overleaf*), or from side buds on underground stems in plants like mint (*right*, not to scale). The gardener usually

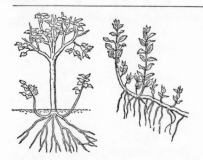

worries about suckers which arise from the roots of grafted or budded shrubs or trees—lilacs, roses, plums, rhododendrons, viburnums may all be grafted and be prone to this trouble. Because they come from the roots suckers have the character of the stock, usually chosen for vigour, and not of the scion, which is the desirable flowering part. If suckers are allowed to grow they may eventually swamp the scion growth entirely, and the plant is then accused of reverting to the stock. Suckers on grafted plants must therefore be removed as soon as possible, and if practicable flush with the root from which they grow. Suckers are sometimes the result of damaging the roots when planting: each wound forms a callus at which adventitious buds can form.

Where the plant is not grafted suckers may still be a nuisance, forming a thicket of growth around the original trunk. In such cases they can provide useful propagating material—raspberries are increased in this way, and also ornamental shrubs such as *Rhus typhina*. *See also* Adventitious; Budding; Callus; Grafting; Reversion; Scion.

SUFFRUTICOSE. *See* Sub-Shrubby.

SYMBIOSIS. The word symbiosis (adjective symbiotic) is derived from Greek words meaning to live together, and refers to the partnership of two distinct living organisms to the benefit of each. Sometimes, as in lichens, the partnership is so complete that a new entity is formed, for a lichen is composed of a fungus and an alga closely united. In most cases, however, the two partners have a separate existence. Thus the nitrogen-fixing bacteria which inhabit the nodules of leguminous plants can live alone in the soil.

The same applies to the main group of symbiotic plants, the fungi. Many of these live in association with roots of other plants; the benefits appear to be mainly derived by the latter, though presumably the fungus gets something out of it. Some plants, notably almost all orchids, cannot grow properly in nature, nor in many cases even germinate, without the association of a certain kind of fungus. Many trees, mainly but by no means only conifers, grow remarkably better in association with fungi, especially as seedlings. These are 'macro-fungi'—what are commonly called toadstools—and a wide range of them form associations with trees, and will be seen growing around them (*left*). In the typical tree/fungus association the tree roots will become short and stubby—coral-like, in fact (*right*, enlarged)—and are surrounded by a layer of fungus cells. The roots have no root-hairs, and the fungus strands permeate them, though without penetrating the root cells. These tree/fungus roots are called mycorrhiza. In fungus associations with orchids and herbaceous plants the fungus usually penetrates the root cells. In both cases the roots receive their nourishment entirely via the fungus. Such activities must not of course be confused with attacks by parasitic fungi such as the deadly bracket fungi or the honey fungus on trees. Even the latter, however, forms a beneficial association with a Japanese terrestrial orchid, which cannot flower without the fungus. *See also* Fungus; Saprophyte.

SYSTEMIC. During recent years a number of systemic insecticides have been produced. These differ from ordinary insecticides in that they are absorbed by the plant, either through the roots or the foliage, or both, and circulate in the sap. This means that only insects which actually feed on the plant's sap are destroyed (*right*), whereas ordinary contact sprays affect all insects which they touch, or which later walk on the sprayed surface, whether they are harmful or beneficial predators such as ladybirds (*left*). Systemics are thus theoretically ideal insect-killing materials, but unfortunately most of those so far produced are very poisonous to warm-blooded animals. Most of them decompose after a few weeks, but—apart from danger while spraying—it is obviously essential to make sure that no vegetable or fruit is eaten within a specific time after spraying. Systemic fungicides also exist.

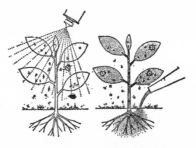

TAKE. The commonest horticultural meaning of take is the same as strike or root—a cutting is said to have 'taken' when it has successfully formed roots and is growing away satisfactorily.

99

Chrysanthemum growers some-times use the word in a rather confusing way. They speak of 'taking' the bud which they wish to retain, which is in fact carried out by the removal of all surplus buds and growths (see sketch: all lower buds are being removed to 'take' or retain the topmost). In fact 'taking' a chrysanthemum bud is best described as disbudding. *See also* Disbudding; Strike.

TAP ROOT. Any strong root growing more or less vertically downwards is called a tap root, though this term is sometimes held to apply only to the first undivided root of a seedling. Plants which normally make tap roots are usually deep feeders as opposed to those surface feeders which have laterally branching roots. Tap roots are presumably so called because they tap deep levels of water. The sea holly (eryngium) is an example of a plant that grows in sand, with water far below, and may have a tap root eight feet long.

In some cases the tap root becomes swollen as a food reserve, and some of this type are vegetables prized for their edible tap roots,

such as carrots, parsnips and scorzonera (illustrated); others, like dandelions and dock, are detested for theirs, because they are too easily broken off and can sprout again from the piece left in the soil. Some gardeners believe it desirable to break the tap roots of brassicas, wall-flowers and related plants by early transplanting, so as to make them produce branching roots; and tradition suggests also the removal of tap roots on unfruitful fruit trees, though whether there is any actual connection between lush unfruitful growth and the presence of a tap root is open to doubt. Certain trees habitually produce tap roots, notably conifers.

TENDER. The word tender, in a horticultural sense, is a vague one. Basically it means a plant that is liable to injury by frost, or at any rate to the cold experienced during an average winter. However, plants which might be described as tender in east England may well survive the winter in the Scillies, Cornwall or on the west coast of Scotland warmed by the Gulf Stream, so the term is a relative one. Moreover, the plant's stage of growth may be involved: thus an old, woody plant well established will often survive a bad winter better than a young sappy one; young growth made in early spring is

also liable to damage. Plants in active growth and full of moisture are more liable to frost damage than those kept relatively dry. In many cases it is a combination of cold and damp that kills plants: thus woolly leaved alpines often succumb to our winters, but no one could call them anything but hardy when in nature they spend the winter covered with snow. For exactly the same reason the word 'hardy' is equally a vague one.

Simple protective measures such as a pane of glass fixed over them will keep alpines from wet, while a piece of sacking fastened round a plant on a wigwam of canes (illustrated), a layer of straw tied round, or even a protective wattle screen, will protect tender plants from cold, and from the searing winds which are especially harmful to young growth in spring. *See also* Hardy.

TENDRIL. Some climbing plants support themselves by organs called tendrils, the simplest of which are thread-like, as in the passion flower (*right*); these move in the air until they touch some solid object, when they coil spirally around it. Vines such as Virginia creepers (*centre*) have tendrils which terminate in little adhesive suckers which will fasten on to a solid surface.

In some cases, like *Clematis alpina* (*left*), the leaf-stalk (petiole) acts as a tendril, forming a loop around any suitable support it encounters. Botanically tendrils may be modified leaves or leaflets, or modified shoots.

TERMINAL. This rather self-explanatory term is frequently used to refer to the uppermost, and usually central, bud, flower or growth on a stem. It is often important, especially when growing flowers for show, to retain only the terminal bud and to remove the subsidiary or lateral buds. In the sketch the terminal dahlia bud is the one in the centre; the others should be nipped out if a large bloom is wanted. *See also* Disbudding.

TERRARIUM. *See* Wardian Case.

TETRAPLOID. Most plants have two sets of chromosomes, the microscopic character-controlling bodies in the cells, and are known

as diploids to the plant breeder. Variations in this number occur for various reasons. When four sets occur, which may be due to a natural sport (mutation) or to artificial treatment as with radiation or colchicine, the plant is described as a tetraploid. Such plants very often have greatly increased vigour. The sketch shows a strain of tetraploid antirrhinums known as Tetra-snaps, large and compact, compared with an ordinary diploid strain. *See also* Chromosome; Sport.

THINNING. The most general meaning of thinning is the reduction of the number of plants in a bed, box or other place, so as to allow those which remain plenty of space and prevent all the plants becoming spindly and weak. This is essential with seedlings of all kinds, unless sown singly, especially when the plants are to mature where sown, and should be carried out at the earliest possible moment that the seedlings are large enough to handle. Early thinning also helps to ensure that the remaining plants are disturbed as little as possible. Thinning is usually carried out by hand, but may be done with a hoe. It is also known as singling.

Thinning on a different scale is sometimes carried out in orchards and forest plantations: as the trees grow, alternate trees, known as fillers, are often removed after some years.

Thinning of shoots is necessary to obtain best results with vigorous perennials, and thinning branches on fruit and ornamental trees may be desirable if they become overcrowded. Thinning is also important with many kinds of fruit, to prevent over-cropping and, more important, to produce fruits of good size which will not be misshapen by pressing on each other in the cluster. Grapes should likewise be thinned as they mature, for which purpose scissors are used.

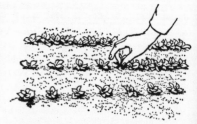

THORN. *See* Spine.

TINE. Each individual prong, spike or tooth on a cultivating tool such as a fork, rake or harrow. Hand-forks may have flat (*left*) or round (*centre*) tines. A special type, known as a hollow-tine fork (*right*), has hollow, round prongs with a slit on one surface, and is used for aerating lawns. The soil is pushed out of the slits on each successive insertion of the fork. The blades of rotary cultivating tools are sometimes loosely called tines.

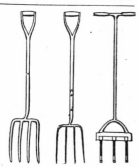

TIP BEARER. A few varieties of fruit tree, notably the apple Worcester Pearmain, produce fruit buds mainly on the tips of one-year-old (and older) shoots, and are known as tip bearers, Such varieties are therefore not very suitable for growing in strictly trained forms such as cordons or espaliers, as the pruning which is normally employed to produce spurs would remove all the fruit buds.

TOOTHED. Many leaves are more or less toothed at the edges, and the shape and size of the teeth are often useful for identification. The Latin equivalent to toothed is dentate (*left*), and usually refers botanically to regular divisions. When angled like the teeth of a circular saw the divisions are called serrate (*left, centre*); when there are small teeth on the main ones, this is called doubly serrate or bi-serrate (*right, centre*). Crenate (*right*) refers to rounded teeth. The terms serrulate and crenulate indicate leaves with small sharp or rounded teeth.

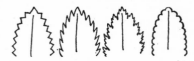

TOMENTOSE. Woolly. *See* Hairy.

TOP DRESSING. This word either refers to the scattering of fertilisers or other substances on to the soil surface without working them in, or to replacing the top inch or so of the soil in pots or tubs with a rich compost, a practice carried out when it is desirable to leave a plant in its container for several years, as with many bulbs and with fruit trees. *See also* Mulch.

TOP-SOIL. *See* Trenching.

TOPIARY. Topiary is the very ancient art—first practised by the Romans over 2000 years ago—of clipping and training shrubs and trees into all kinds of shapes, from more complicated hedges to single specimens representing cones, balls, pyramids, peacocks, and other birds and beasts. The great era of topiary in this country was

the seventeenth century. Many plants can be used for topiary, the favourites being yew and box. Shaping should if possible begin when the plants are young, and is carried out by trimming with shears or secateurs and also by tying selected young growths into position, until they are stout enough to retain the position required on their own. In complex specimens a wire frame may be used, which remains in place but becomes completely concealed as the specimen matures.

TOPPING. A word used rather loosely to indicate removal of the top of a plant. Though really meaning the same as stopping, the latter is usually done to make the plant produce side growths; topping is done for some other purpose, such as that illustrated, the removal of the top of a broad bean plant, which is liable to become infested with black aphis in late spring. Topping also refers to the removal of the top of a tree. *See also* Stopping.

TRENCHING. Trenching is a very thorough method of digging in which the soil is cultivated to a depth of 30 inches. To begin trenching a trench one spit deep (about 10 inches) and three feet wide is made, the soil being taken to the other end of the plot (1). Next, this trench is divided lengthwise and the soil from one half dug out another spit deep (2). This is also removed to the end of the plot, but kept separate from the first heap. This 18 in. wide trench is now broken up with a fork to the fork's depth (3). Following this the undug part of the second spit soil is turned over on to the forked sub-soil (4), and the exposed sub-soil is forked in its turn (5). A new strip of top-soil, 18 inches wide, is now marked out, and the top-soil is dug on to the step of second spit soil in the first trench (6). The sub-soil in the new trench is turned into the first trench (7), the sub-soil forked (8), and the sequence repeated on a new 18 in. strip. The heaps of top and second spit soil originally removed are replaced at the appropriate levels at the end of the operation. It is usually important to keep sub-soil below top-soil, as it normally lacks organic matter, bacteria and good growing qualities. Of course the top-soil may be deeper than two or three spits, but this is unusual.

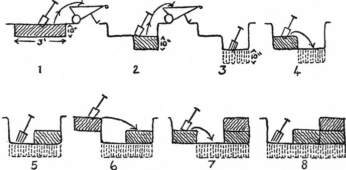

A trench as such is sometimes used for certain crops, such as runner beans, leeks, celery and sweet peas. The soil in a narrow strip is deeply cultivated and manure or compost worked into it. In this way plenty of nourishment is concentrated in friable soil around the plant roots. In heavy soils, however, this method has the disadvantage that the trench may act as a sump and become waterlogged. *See also* Spit.

TRIPLOID. A triploid is an organism with one and a half times the normal complement of chromosomes (the microscopic bodies in cell nuclei which transmit hereditary characters). This triploid situation, usually abbreviated technically as 3x, sometimes arises in hybrids or mutations. Like other polyploids (plants with more than the normal number of chromosomes), triploids may have bigger flowers or fruits than normal; but triploid fruit trees have less fertile pollen than normal ones, and thus it is wise to plant other suitable trees to fertilise their flowers. Examples are the apples Blenheim Orange and Bramley's Seedling (illustrated). *See also* Chromosome.

TRUMPET. A rather self-evident word, trumpet is not really a botanical term, but is often used to describe flowers which resemble a trumpet in shape. The plant illustrated, *Campsis radicans*, is called the Trumpet Vine, and its flowers are typically trumpet-shaped; but the word is sometimes applied also to narrowly cone-shaped blooms (*see* Corolla for illustration). The word is also used in connection with daffodils, which are known as trumpet varieties when the corona is as long as, or longer than, the perianth segments. Division I of the official narcissus classification is composed of trumpet narcissi. *See also* Corona; Cup.

 **TRUNCATE.** The word truncate is the technical way of writing truncated, and in botany indicates a part of a plant, usually a leaf, which looks as if its tip has been cut off more or less flat. The leaf of the tulip tree, *Liriodendron tulipifera* (illustrated), is an example. The word is sometimes Latinised, as in Zygocactus truncatus, the Christmas cactus, where it refers to the cut-off appearance of the flat-ended leaf-like stem segments.

TRUSS. A rather loose, non-botanical term denoting a cluster of flowers or fruits. One often speaks of a truss of tomatoes (*left*), but not of a truss of grapes. The term is probably best restricted to compact flower-clusters at the ends of stems, like those of rhododendrons (*right*) or phloxes.

TUBE. A self-explanatory term referring to the long tubular section which sometimes occurs on a flower between its base and the

perianth segments. A typical example is in cacti of the epiphyllum group (illustrated), in which a long tube is an identification feature. Such a tube is in no sense a stem, for the style, if not always the stamens, will pass right down it to the ovary at its base.

TUBER. A tuber is a swollen stem or root, usually but not invariably underground, which is used for the storage of food during a resting season. In this it much resembles the corm, though this usually has a membranous coat (e.g. crocuses). Tubers

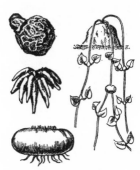

may be stem tubers when they have eyes or buds, as in *Anemone coronaria* (*top, left*), cyclamen (*below, left*) and potato; and root tubers when they do not, as in the Persian ranunculus (*centre, left*) and dahlia—in these growth springs from a crown, the individual tubers being incapable of producing buds. Tubers are occasionally seen in succulents such as *Ceropegia woodii* (*right*), which forms small tubers on the stems, and eventually a larger one at the base. *See also* Crown.

UMBEL, UMBELLIFER. An umbel is an inflorescence, or flower-head, in which the individual flower stems (peduncles) arise from a common point, as in an umbrella.

These flower stems are sometimes known as rays. The umbel is the characteristic shape of the inflorescence in the family *Umbelliferae* (cow parsley, carrot, etc.), in which each main ray usually branches into another set of smaller rays which support the flowers, as in the caraway (illustrated in seed for clarity). Umbels are also occasionally found on other familes.

UNDULATE. A word meaning wavy, applied usually to leaves with wavy margins, as in *Veltheimia viridiflora* (illustrated), but also sometimes to petals, as in some nerines. The waviness applies to up-and-down

107

undulations, not to in-and-out ones which might be called scalloped, crenate, and so on. The word is sometimes Latinised in a specific name, as in *Verbascum undulatum.*

VARIEGATED. A great number of plants are variegated, a term which is usually confined to white or cream markings on the foliage as opposed to marks of brown, red or other dark colours due to pigmentation. Variegation is in a sense the opposite of pigmentation, being usually due to an absence of chlorophyll (the basic green colouring matter of the leaf). Few species begin life with variegation, though sometimes it is 'built in', as in Pilea cadierei (c) in which the aluminium-coloured markings are the result of air spaces beneath the surface.

Very often variegation is the result of a mutation (sport) which creates a chimaera in which tissues of two or more kinds occur, one often overlying the other. Pelargoniums (e) are very liable to this sort of marking, often in several colours, and the longitudinal variegations on leaves like those of dracaenas (b) are usually chimaeras. Longitudinal or edge variegation is the most common, but rarely leaves are striped horizontally, as in the zebra rush, *Scirpus tabernaemontani zebrinus* (a).

Variegation in the form of spots is often a symptom of virus infection; one of the most frequent plant viruses is known as mosaic because of its appearance. Virus-caused variegations are seldom prized in the garden, but the 'broken' tulips are notable exceptions, while *Ligularia kaempferi aureo-maculata* (d) is sometimes grown as a foliage plant.

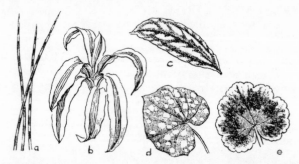

Variegated plants can normally only be increased vegetatively, and are often weaker than their original green counterparts, to which they may revert, as they are often unstable. *See also* Chimaera; Feathered; Sport; Virus.

VARIETY. In the horticultural sense the word variety refers to any plant with distinctive features, desirable for its decorative, culinary or other properties, which can be reproduced true either vegetatively or from seed. Natural species may themselves produce varieties, which may, for instance, have double, larger or more brilliant flowers than the original; otherwise varieties are produced by active selection or breeding by man and in many cases differ enormously from the original species. The illustration shows the original species of *Freesia refracta* (*top*, *left*), a variety with much larger and more numerous flowers, evolved by

selection (*top*, *right*), and the recent double form produced by breeding (*below*). The official word for a horticultural variety is cultivar. *See also* Genus; Strain.

VEGETATIVE. *See* Clone; Propagation.

VERNALISATION. This term covers various techniques by which seeds, bulbs and also plants will start rapidly into growth, out of season, as soon as provided with adequate light, warmth and moisture. The word, meaning literally 'subjecting to spring', is really a misnomer, for the techniques actually subject the seed or bulb to the conditions they would normally receive in winter, and so speed up, or produce at an abnormal time of year, the physical and chemical changes which then occur. It is, in effect, an artificial breaking of dormancy.

Such techniques are widely applied to bulbs for very early forcing, which are described as 'specially prepared', and also to lily-of-the-valley. The exposure to frost of sea-kale, rhubarb and similar roots for forcing beforehand is another example.

Seeds can also be made to germinate at abnormal times by vernalisation, and the original experiments in Russia concerned winter wheat, which if sown in early winter produced bigger crops than normal varieties, but if sown in spring failed to form ears at all. If the winter varieties are germinated at low temperatures and stored cold till sown in spring they will produce ears in the normal way. Many seeds, notably and obviously those of alpines, and of most temperate-climate plants, need a period of chilling before they will germinate—easily provided in a domestic refrigerator.

Vernalisation usually means temperature treatment, sometimes cold as described above, sometimes warmth, as with seeds of warm-country plants, and bulbs such as hyacinths in which flower formation occurs during the resting or storage period (as opposed to daffodils in which flower formation in the bulb happens when the plant is still in growth in relatively cool conditions). Certain chemicals, notably gibberellic acid, can be used to the same ends, and day-length may also affect matters. *See also* Forcing.

VERTICEL. *See* Whorl.

VILLOUS. *See* Hairy.

VIRUS. The name virus is applied to a large number of disease-causing organisms which are distinct from fungi and bacteria. They are far smaller, and their mode of life is not properly understood. They are extremely infectious and multiply rapidly in suitable conditions, which are usually to be found in the sap of plants. Recently it has been found that some viruses exist in the soil and can infect the roots directly, but most are transmitted by sap-sucking insects, occasionally by birds and also by human activity, such as on grafting knives or on fingers, as when removing side shoots on tomatoes. One of the most important series of viruses, the nicotiana viruses, which affect tomatoes and many other plants, can be transmitted by finger contact from smoking tobacco or cigarettes to plants.

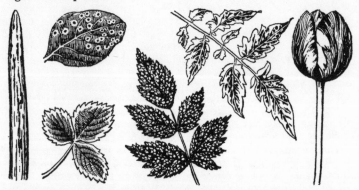

Viruses attack almost every kind of plant and cause a wide variety of symptoms, especially kinds of mottling and streaking. Some of these are illustrated above: *from left to right*, a narcissus virus, a tobacco virus (*above*), strawberry yellow edge (*below*), raspberry mosaic, tomato spotted wilt and finally a 'broken' tulip, one of the few viruses encouraged by gardeners. Besides such markings viruses may distort stems and foliage or stunt plants, and they all weaken the victim in some degree.

In some cases viruses do not produce visible symptoms, though they can be detected by laboratory tests. Most fruit trees carry such invisible viruses, which often reduce cropping capacity, though in the normal course of events this will not be suspected.

Because of their character viruses cannot be destroyed by applying chemicals as one does against fungus diseases. With some plants, such as strawberries, heat treatment is possible, while in chrysanthemums and other plants this may be combined with a special technique of rooting tiny tip cuttings or making microscopic grafts. Such methods are beyond the amateur, though he can benefit from them by purchasing guaranteed virus-free stocks produced in such ways. The amateur's only hope of control is stringent war against sap-sucking insects, special care when handling plants such as tomatoes, cucumbers and melons which need deshooting, and speedy destruction of virus-infected plants. *See also* Feathered; Reversion; Variegated.

VIVIPAROUS. In the animal kingdom, viviparous means bringing forth live young. The only viviparous creature the gardener has to contend with is the aphis in its various forms, and he has to remember that even when killed by an insecticide an adult aphis can still produce live young, so that it is wise to repeat applications after a few days.

When applied to plants, viviparous refers, strictly speaking, to seeds which germinate naturally when still attached to the parent, as in the mangrove. It is also used to describe certain plants which produce youngsters without recourse to seeds. An example is *Saxifraga cernua* (*left*) which produces a false 'flower' head composed of vegetative buds. When they become detached from the parent they grow into new plants. In the fern Asplenium bulbiferum (*right*) similar buds appear on the fronds. Other plants which can be called viviparous—another word is proliferous—include some succulent bryophyllums, which produce infant plants on the leaves (*see* Adventitious for illustration).

It is interesting that this phenomenon is most common in alpine and arctic plants, such as the saxifrage illustrated, which have only a short growing season and in a bad year may be unable to ripen seeds.

WARDIAN CASE. In 1829, by chance, a Dr Nathaniel Ward discovered that plants would thrive in completely closed glass containers, the moisture transpired by the plant condensing and returning to the soil. In a short time Ward's Cases became fashionable and they were produced in a wide range of ornate shapes, such as the one illustrated (*left*). Sometimes they were immense, and contained rockwork, like one famous type representing the ruins of Tintern Abbey. Simple, box-like cases solved the problems of collectors sending plants to Britain from far countries.

The Wardian Case is still an excellent method for the cultivation of difficult plants indoors—plants which must have humid atmosphere and shrivel up in the dry, stuffy air of the average room. Though it is not possible to buy a Wardian Case today a box-like one (*below, right*) is easily manufactured at home. Such a case could if desired be heated by soil-warming wires or placed over a radiator. The most decorative form of Wardian Case is undoubtedly the bottle garden (*above, right*); any large bottle can be used, but the carboy shown is ideal. A couple of long canes and a piece of flat wood strip are the only essential tools, and putting plants in is easier than it might appear. In America such cases are called terrariums.

WAVY. *See* Undulate.

WATER SHOOTS. Water shoots are growths which often arise on vigorously growing fruit trees from adventitious buds in the branches. They are long, stout and quick-growing, quite distinct from spurs, and are encouraged by hard pruning

and good soils. Since they are unfruitful, soft, and ill-placed, crowding the centre of the tree, they should be cut off at the base, flush with the branch. *See also* Adventitious; Snag.

WEEPING. Many trees have varieties of weeping or pendulous habit, which mainly arise as sports (mutations) and, used in the right place, they make very attractive garden features. Naturally weeping trees include the weeping willow, *Salix babylonica*, the silver lime, *Tilia petiolaris*, and *Forsythia suspensa*. There are some

trees where the weeping is confined to the twigs, as in *Picea breweriana* in which the secondary growths hang vertically from the branches. The weeping willow, and certain weeping varieties of ash and beech, are examples of trees which form an erect trunk from which the branches hang down, but in most cases of weeping sports it is necessary to train a growth upward to form an erect trunk, as in *Cedrus atlantica pendula* (*left*). In other cases the weeping sport is grafted on to the erect stem of the original species; if it was not so treated it would make a prostrate or sprawling bush. This usually happens with weeping cherries, and indeed most weeping trees. Weeping standard roses are another example where pendulous or at least weak-stemmed varieties are budded on to an upright stock: with these it is usual to use an umbrella-shaped frame (*right*) over which the long growths are trained. *See also* Grafting; Scion; Sport.

WHORL. When three or more flowers or leaves appear at one stem node in a circle the formation is botanically known as a whorl or verticil (adjective verticillate). The candelabra primulas such as *P. pulverulenta* (illustrated) are good examples of flowers in verticillate arrangement.

113

WING. Botanically the term wing is applied to a flat appendage to some part of a plant. Apart from such appendages which are literally wings, like those on a sycamore seed, certain plants have wings along the stems, as in *Euonymus alatus*, or on the seeds, as in the asparagus pea, *Tetragonolobus purpureus* (illustrated). The word alate is derived from the Latin for wing, and is sometimes used in specific names as above. The other meaning of wing in botany is in referring to the side petals of the sweet pea and other papilionaceous flowers of the pea family. *See also* Leguminous.

WITCH'S BROOM. Witches' brooms are the thick clusters of twiggy growth sometimes to be found on almost all kinds of tree. Though sometimes the result of branch sports (mutations) these growths are usually the result of infection by a fungus. The type of growth caused by the same fungus on the same tree can show extraordinary variation; the fungus presumably causes the genetical structure of the tree's cell nuclei to alter locally in different ways, but how this occurs is a complete mystery. Witches' brooms can be treated as cuttings, just as can any other parts of the tree concerned, and once on their own roots the resulting plants remain dwarf. The majority of dwarf conifers are the result of rooting witches' brooms. *See also* Fungus; Sport.

XEROPHYTE. Derived from the Greek words for dry and plant, a xerophyte is a plant adapted to living in arid conditions, or in places where the water supply is limited to short seasons. The obvious examples are cacti and other succulents, which store water in fleshy stems or leaves: but many other plants have adaptations to this end, notably leaves reduced in size and number, sometimes disappearing altogether, leaves rolled up, branches reduced to thorns, and thick cuticles or waxy or hairy coverings. This is often combined with a great reduction in the number of stomata (breathing pores) and their protection from hot air and drying winds—which would encourage loss of moisture by transpiration—

by being buried in pits or by the shape of the leaf; the rolling of many grass leaves provides an example of the latter. The illustrations show, *left*, *Astragalus spinosus*, one of the many members of the pea family which have developed spines due to arid conditions; in this case the leaf-bearing branches become spines as they age. *Centre* is another pea, the Spanish broom, *Spartium junceum*, in

which the leaves are greatly reduced, their functions being taken over by the hard green stems. *Right* is the oleander, *Nerium oleander*, with very leathery leaves, the stomata of which are hidden in pits (enlarged section of leaf, *below*). *See also* Cactus; Spine; Stomata; Succulent.

ZYGOMORPHIC. A word applied to irregular flowers (i.e. those in which there are parts of different shape) which can be divided into symmetrical halves only in the vertical plane, as in the pea, snapdragon, schizanthus or Peruvian lily (alstroemeria). The illustrated example is the striking amaryllid *Sprekelia formosissima*, the Jacobean lily.